LEAVING
A TRACE

Also by Alexandra Johnson

The Hidden Writer:
Diaries and the Creative Life

LEAVING A TRACE

On Keeping a Journal

*The Art of Transforming
a Life into Stories*

Alexandra Johnson

Little, Brown and Company
Boston New York London

First Edition

Library of Congress Cataloging-in-Publication Data

Johnson, Alexandra.
    Leaving a trace: on keeping a journal : the art of transforming a life into stories / Alexandra Johnson. — 1st ed.
        p. cm.
    ISBN 0-316-12020-0
        1. Diaries — History and criticism. 2. Diaries — Authorship. I. Title.

PN4390.J55 2001
808'.06692 — dc21

                                                            00-042843

10   9   8   7   6   5   4   3   2   1

Q-FF

Text design by Meryl Sussman Levavi/Digitext
Printed in the United States of America

For my grandmother Florence

Contents

∽

PART THREE

*Crossover: Moving a Journal into
Creative Work*

LEAVING
A TRACE

All serious daring starts within.

— EUDORA WELTY

There looms ahead of me the shadow of some kind of form which the diary might attain. I might in the course of time learn what it is that one can make of this loose, drifting material of life; finding another use for it.

— VIRGINIA WOOLF

Introduction

❧

New Year's Day, Tuesday, Jan 1st. I think I will try to keep a diary this year.

I stared at that sentence one autumn afternoon, holding a stranger's diary in my hands. It was a soft-cover exercise book, chosen, I'm sure, so no one would suspect it was a diary and be tempted to read it. But I was and I did. With each page, a stranger's life slowly unfolded: waiting for someone named Charlie to return from college; having her ice skates sharpened at a nearby frozen pond; going into Boston with her sister Mattie to buy sheet music; celebrating her twenty-first birthday, glad the absent young man had sent violets that survived a snowstorm.

I was given the diary by the sole survivor of a family who had known the woman. The woman who kept the journal, I was told, had lived in the house I now own. A woman, I now saw in my imagination, who once climbed the same narrow flight of stairs each night and who looked out at our two pear trees still bearing fruit. A woman who wrote in her diary in 1895, plotting her life in sepia ink.

Could she have imagined how a century later someone in her own house would be fascinated by the clues she left of a life that probably seemed immensely dull to her at the time? (I imagined her scribbling in the journal like homework, the task vaguely self-improving.) Was it her only diary? Or did she burn later ones? I needed to know: What happened late that summer of 1895? Did Charlie vanish? How did he finally break her heart? I hoped that heartbreak wasn't lurking in the unexpected: those pale gray eyes of her close friend Kitty. Toward the diary's end the handwriting is frantic — the loops of the l's swell like lungs bursting.

As I closed Elizabeth Howe's diary, I thought about how, if we can't keep diaries ourselves, we still love reading others', eavesdropping on lives in private conversation with themselves. With each page I watched Howe try to find a narrative shape for her life, a way to tell its story, if only to herself. In stolen private moments, her hand recorded what I'm sure her brain constantly told her was of no importance: her life. From her journal I knew hers was a quiet but hungrily alive life. The pages chronicled a twenty-one-year-old music teacher secretly thrilled by solitude, love letters, fresh peaches wrapped in tissue, ice storms filigreeing the windows at night with crystal spiderwebs.

Those details from her diary lingered in my mind all afternoon. But I found that one nagged in particular. To earn pocket money, Elizabeth Howe and her sister spent a mild May afternoon copying names from gravestones into a ledger; the cemetery was soon to be relocated. On that bright spring day, she noted, the air was "sharp with lilac." It was a change from bitter winters whose winds had eroded so many tombstones. To trace the oldest names, she ran her fingers over the hollowed grooves, like Braille. I wondered as she traced those ancient New England names, copied for pennies a name, if she was haunted by how many had been lost to memory. Here were lives as blank as their slate markers. The next day, her diary stops its complaining. The entries are longer. Suddenly, the pages question if she has talent as a pianist. Or, as she wondered in her journal, was her destiny instructing thankless pupils forever?

I'll never know the answers. But as she copied name after name, I'm sure she couldn't help wondering about those lives, just as I did about hers now. What had been their ambitions, regrets, last thoughts, deepest earthly pleasures? What illnesses had they survived? How many safe childbirths? Whose name was the last they called out for? (I picture her bent over the ledger lost in thought, her chestnut hair so shiny you could see your reflection in it.) "Seven headstones too hard to read," she noted that night in the journal, disturbed by those unclaimed lives. Knowing what each had accomplished within a life was as hard as guessing the color of their eyes.

I placed her thin exercise book on a shelf in the same room where I write this now. It sits up high, near a number of the same novels her journal records her reading on long summer nights — *Wuthering Heights, David Copperfield, Silas Marner*. I like to think she wrote secretly in her diary here. Since then, this room's shelves have filled with other diaries and journals, a good many of them published, some sent to me while I wrote this book. My hand, like a dowsing rod, goes to them during dry seasons: to console, to inspire, to remind me how others used a diary to deepen a life, or negotiate the obstacle course of creativity.

On the same shelf where Elizabeth Howe's journal now sits are a half-dozen notebooks I kept at her same age. On the first page of the earliest notebook, I'd copied a diary entry from Virginia Woolf, whose novels and diaries claim an entire shelf of their own. At thirty-four, a newly inspired Woolf started keeping a diary once again.

> What sort of diary should I like mine to be? Something loose knit and yet not slovenly, so elastic that it will embrace any thing, solemn, slight or beautiful that comes into my mind. I should like it to resemble some deep old desk, or capacious hold-all, in which one flings a mass of odds and ends without looking. I should like to come back, after a year or two, and find that the collection had sorted itself . . . into a mould, transparent enough to reflect the light of our life.

Hers would. Until four days before her death, at sixty, she wrote in more than thirty-two marble patterned notebooks, leaving one of the most complete records of a creative mind at work. Woolf kept diaries, in part, to give her something to read at fifty. At twenty-one, when I copied that passage from her diary, I hoped that whatever I wrote in my notebook would sort itself out without my help. It didn't. The journals remained either stubbornly blank or feverish with introspection that seemed curiously unreflective. (How to tell one year from the next, the entries so moody and abstract in their complaints? "Once again I can't believe that . . . Why it is that I always . . .") Instead, I'd find myself filling journals with the sharper, polished wisdoms of writers like Woolf. "All strong emotion leaves its indelible mark," I copied out, "and it is only a question of discovering how we can get ourselves again attached to it, so that we shall be able to live our lives through from the start." The past, Virginia Woolf noted, urges us to "leave a trace."

Isn't this secretly what we try for yet fear we'll never achieve? This instinct to leave a trace is a story I know all too well. I've been watching it since childhood. My grandmother, an American Red Cross worker in Siberia, kept a visual journal of war relief in Vladivostok, pasting in photos, letters, and the now-faded telegram in which my grandfather proposed. My mother hid her own weepy, complaining journals in the linen closet. (Cotton sheets, freshly ironed, often trigger my memory of finding those scraps of paper. I recall first seeing her familiar handwriting scribbled on the back of foreign airmail envelopes. In between their red-and-blue-bordered edges, my mother mapped some inner geography of desire — a lust for privacy, secret thoughts on her marriage.) Her older sister, between teaching and raising three children, kept journals for novels she'd write but was too terrified to send off.

These three generations within my own family show the range of what is possible in a journal: my grandmother, the chronicler, kept her visual diary to record a public life; my mother kept a private journal of inner life to reflect, often to vent, or clarify; my aunt used a journal as a springboard into creative work. My own, begun at nine, would play with each of these forms before finding its true shape in my late twenties.

The open secret of my childhood: I had filled only twenty pages in the vinyl drugstore diary I'd coerced my mother into buying one hot July when I was nine. Between ten and eleven, I made no progress. Each new diary was suspended in late January, doomed to a limbo of New Year's resolutions. Between pink vinyl covers, I practiced penmanship, my increasingly sturdy diagonals mocking me, since the pages were still often blank, as if I were illiterate. At twelve, I stared hard at what I'd managed to record. Was it possible that my life was really *that* boring? The proof was incriminatingly kept in my own hand, entries dated as regularly as a prison lockup. The litany of daily life reads as flat as the lines that guided my ballpoint: "school; walked dog; dinner — mashed potatoes, frozen peas, baked meatloaf, ketchup bled into rim of Pyrex pan."

The most shaming are days where there's that single entry: "nothing." Nothing? Yet in memory, I can still summon those afternoons: playing outside as dusk fell, turning my shorts whiter in the darkening light; the sharp sting of eucalyptus trees; sitting on the cool linoleum of the school library, a sticky rectangle of a Band-Aid on my knee, as I first discovered books I'd love, like Anne Frank's diary. Only occasionally in the diaries is there a pulse of something true: my friend Diane Friedman and I hoarding candy from girls who'd refused to sit with us; the murderous envy I felt for Nancy Miller's new biscuit-colored shoes; the strange wistfulness of hearing my brother alone in nearby hills shooting a BB gun.

By contrast, my family's journals, however haphazardly kept, pulsated with the exotic. To unlock their secrets, I'd pore over the black, cardboard-thick album pages of my grandmother's Siberian journal, staring at photos of her in surgical garb. In silver pencil, she'd written "Vladivostok" or "wounded transport prisoners" beneath grainy photos of Russian soldiers, their feet swaddled in bandages. The album ends in Brooklyn, New York, where she lived and did prenatal medical care, too busy to keep journals with a baby of her own on the way.

But I suspected that, like the black triangular grips holding the photos in place, there were blanks, small black holes behind these preserved images. If my

8

diaries were boring from the sheer terminal me-ness of them, I suspected hers meant to record but also to remain invisible. It was her only journal, a visual scrapbook whose few words leave no trace of her life before then. That stubby silver pencil would never tell the hidden story I knew only in fragments: orphaned at two, paraded in family court at six, unclaimed. I wanted to probe the mystery of her background. It seemed as hidden as her medical whites under that heavy Red Cross cape, as if her life only began with that long sea voyage to Japan and Russia. Unknowingly, as I flipped through her album journal, I was taking in my first lessons in fiction.

While I didn't then want to know the confessed facts of my mother's marriage, I admired my aunt's instinct to transform her longings into imagined stories. After a full day's work and putting children to bed, she scribbled in journals, imagining plots for novels: heroines trapped in nineteenth-century Alaska, shy schoolteachers turned pioneering fur traders. With each page she made life exotic, the way she felt her suburban world wasn't. (This was the stuff, I thought: getting rid of your boredom simply by giving it to characters!)

"Writing," Kafka jotted in his journal, "is the axe that breaks the frozen sea within." Journals hint at what's long been hidden under the ice. They shimmer with patterns of longing, secrets, untold stories. The diarist plays detective to his own days, uncovering the extraordinary in the ordinary, the truer story beneath the stubbornly recorded fact. (For what is left out is often more interesting than what's chosen, the central dramas often held offstage — love, heartbreak, betrayal.) Yet no matter how incomplete or fitfully kept, journals honor that most human of instincts: our need to leave a trace.

As I write this, my room is filled with others' journals, the floor piled with the many lent me for this book, or with the hundreds of stories that have crossed the threshold of this small, sunlit room. Three years ago, it was the *living* voices I heard that thrilled me while going across country for my first book about writers' diaries. At readings, in workshops, in calls to National Public Radio, they were voices whose current journal stories read like terrific novels: stolen diaries, found lost loves; feuding siblings' secret journals; spouses suicidally sharing a single diary; distant mothers whose inner lives were revealed — and understood — only after death, journals read by family survivors.

Here's what I also heard. It was a phrase mumbled between these stories: *Who could possibly care about my life?* It was said wistfully as I signed books that were being given to encourage someone else — a gifted son, a sister who always kept journals, a recently divorced daughter who now might. But here is what I knew: for every life reduced to ten-word entries in a daily organizer, the pen still maps the epic — work, children, health, love. Even the kitchen calendar whose squares are filled in daily is silently recording the heroic of the everyday. The driest factual record often evokes a history far larger than the life it chronicles — memories of war, the Holocaust, transplanted cultures. And here, finally, is what I saw in face after face: most were lives full of stories or projects they feared would never be set down.

That's why they'd come to sit in an audience or show up at a workshop. I heard hundreds of stories across the country from men and women, eighteen- to eighty-year-olds, beginning and seasoned journal keepers alike. While many were long-term journal keepers, most were not. Their stories were an echo of my own: people who'd been given a diary early in life, going from a child frustrated by poor penmanship to fitful journal keeping in college to adults too busy to keep journals yet hungry to do so. Often they were discouraged when they did. Many found they wrote only when angry or depressed. The richest part of the story was left out. Or, in their eyes, so poorly written. But no matter why, how, or how often they wrote, every single person wanted to leave a trace of a life. For themselves or for others. The ways varied: in the form of a diary, a family chronicle, a memoir. Whether stymied or inspired, they always came back to the same two questions: How do I keep a journal? And: What do I *do* with all the material in the ones I've kept?

This book is a way to honor those and the many other questions I've heard over the years in journal workshops, creative writing classes, and within my own writing group. The solutions to those questions are ones I live daily as a writer sitting at a desk. In writing *Leaving a Trace*, my goal isn't to turn every diarist into a professional writer, but to guide others in how to keep some form of a journal and transform it into larger projects or writing. A diary is the missing link in creative life. In journal and creative nonfiction workshops, I watch journals serve as building blocks, moving from lists to sketches to memoir. Always wait for the surprise, I say, the way a journal opens out a life in unexpected ways. For a former student such as Julie Hilden, it was transforming scraps of recollections into a celebrated published memoir. For a woman I met in Chicago, it was beginning a journal at eighty, finding herself writing poetry at eighty-two, organizing life-story writing groups within nursing homes. For many, the question *How do I keep a journal?* quickly becomes *What do I do with all the material in the ones I've kept?*

My own writing life spans these two questions. I still write as easily on the back of a Visa slip as in a notebook, but what's changed is how I see what a journal can be, reimagining its form, purpose, even the very way I take in the immediate world. Showing the ways that are possible is the subject of this book. Looking back, I see that the clues for me were always there even in abandoned half-filled notebooks. In my early twenties, I wanted to write. Anything. On an October morning, I came across a journal strangely like my own. It was a mess. A scattering of odd-sized, mismatched notebooks, with pages often crosshatched with corrections. Weeks, often months, were skipped between entries. Grocery lists sat next to ideas for future projects, travel notes were jotted next to comments on marriage. Unsent letters were stuck in randomly.

But I read, fascinated, because the diarist, the New Zealand short-story writer Katherine Mansfield, subtly changed her fate through this odd assortment of notebooks. Mansfield, who'd burned "the huge complaining diaries" of her childhood, kept journals for process: to practice craft as much as to clarify thoughts. She used her journals like a small savings account. Out of them came project after project. They are three forms in one:

a writer's notebook, a journal of inner life, a spiritual autobiography.

"I am 33," she wrote. "Yet I'm only just beginning to see now what it is I want to do. It will take years of work to really bring it off. How unbearable it would be to die — leave 'scraps,' 'bits,' nothing really finished." Mansfield died of tuberculosis a year after writing that entry. But not before mining her journal, producing a quarter of her final work in "a race to get in as much as one can before it *disappears*." Notes jotted in doctors' waiting rooms ("My sciatica! Remember to give to someone in a story one day"), the unsent letters, the grocery lists next to characters' names — all had been waiting to be used.

Her journal was a small revelation. (Others also found it so. The only time *The Journal of Katherine Mansfield* has not been in print was when she was actually writing in it.) What makes a great diary, one worth reading over and over? The ways it keeps trying to cut to the ever-shifting core of life, offering clues to how to record and transform our own. At twenty-four, mine changed by reading others' diaries carefully. I began experimenting, imitating, stealing. From Virginia Woolf, I learned how to keep a pen moving, imitating her "haphazard gallop" to avoid self-censorship. From Anne Frank, I learned how to look for patterns in a diary with an eye for imagining larger work. From Emerson, I learned how to index scores of past journals. From da Vinci, I learned how to keep the writing secret.

But most of all what I learned was how to give a journal a specific purpose: a way to focus its content, giving it staying power. As my shelves filled with separate notebooks — travel journals, commonplace books full of quotations, writers' notebooks — so they filled with the work that had come out of them. Now, I never have to worry about getting started. In dry seasons, all I have to do is open an old journal. Inside, something waits — a fact, a memory, a question — to spark a new project. I learned long ago not to care what the journals look like, or if they're well written (they're usually not), or how often I fill the pages.

It's taken time, but the journals taught me. I learned how to play detective to my own days. I learned to uncover the extraordinary in the ordinary in daily life. I learned that just below the surface of quickly jotted facts, there's always a more interesting story waiting to be claimed. I learned that stories often need to wait years in forgotten journals before you can discover how — and when — to tell them.

Leaving a Trace is full of others' stories. Lives of people who, over time, have discovered the innumerable ways a journal can be a stepping-stone. A great many lives will crisscross the chapters. Some are people I know well, others I first met at readings or workshops or in conversation on National Public Radio. Among them: the mathematician who solves complex formulas thanks to ten years of keeping dream journals; the retired lawyer who, at seventy-two, transformed his diary into a unique World War II memoir; the artist being treated for rare brain cancer who used a journal to continue her work while in hospital; the athlete who interrupted graduate studies at Cambridge to record a single year — her final shot to compete in the Olympics; the family scattered over three continents who share a journal; the couple who reseeded a marriage by planning a garden, using a journal to chart its (and their) strange new growth.

While journals often focus on success — from overcoming breast cancer to creating a bestselling memoir — many chart things diarists thought twice about before committing to pages. But these are among the most powerful stories: how a journal helped preserve a woman's hope after falling between life's crevices into ten months of homelessness; how a journal was the first transformative step in lives scarred by neglect or abuse; how discovering journal keeping while staying in a shelter offered one single mother a lifeline of perspective. No matter their content, journals are always recording history. Sometimes it's literal, such as the journal memoir of a woman whose father attempted to assassinate Hitler. More often, though, it comes in a subtler form: an immigrant preserving Old World culture within a strange new one, or a mother with scientific precision keeping a journal of her child's first year.

In the chapters that follow, I often let passages from the actual diaries tell their stories. Others I've woven into my own reflections on how journals help in leaving a trace. Some of the voices are famous but the majority are not. Some diarists began journals at nine, others at eighty. Some write only for their own eyes; others tell you how they moved from private to public voice.

A tall stack of journals sits nearby as I write. At the top is an unusual journal: a month's worth of tiny self-portraits drawn and commented upon by a retired teacher, Lisa Colt. At sixty-seven, she's experiencing a renaissance of late-life work. All of it stems from journals she only began keeping in her late thirties. The habit was sparked by finding a journal kept by one of her ancestors. Hers is a New England family name as old as the ones Elizabeth Howe copied into her ledger that May afternoon. In 1866 a family member glued an iris inside a commonplace book. Nearly 140 years later it's still there, glued above the inscription a wife wrote to honor her husband: "This iris stood in the room where rested the remains of him who planted it."

Journals are a kind of deep planting. Some blossom into a whole garden; others, a single bloom. Since I began writing *Leaving a Trace*, dozens of babies have been born to the book's diarists; several journal keepers have become ill; others have gone into full recovery. Sons and daughters have gone off to college; others finished law or graduate school. Couples have retired. Others grapple in diaries over honoring a parent's wish not to enter a nursing home. Scores of grandchildren and grandparents at this very moment are interviewing each other for family chronicles. Lives quickly change. They are as fragile as those birthday violets Elizabeth Howe's journal recorded as surviving a snowstorm.

The world's most famous diaries, those passed from hand to hand, generation to generation, are often ones sparked by extremity or terrible urgency. Anne Frank in hiding; Katherine Mansfield in illness. Fragments of a diary for a fragment of a life.

But even writing a single journal is a triumph. It, too, leaves an indelible trace.

I keep one such journal next to my bedside: Etty Hillesum's *An Interrupted Life*. Two miles from where

Anne Frank was in hiding in Amsterdam, twenty-seven-year-old Etty Hillesum also kept a diary. Between 1941 and 1943, its pages chronicled her deepest desires — a wish to write, to be loved, to know God. At its heart, it celebrates a timeless search for meaning while carefully recording all that would extinguish it. Hillesum perished at Auschwitz when she was twenty-nine. But not before leaving behind one of the twentieth century's great diaries, an original voice whose courage burns steady as a wick.

"All that words should do," she wrote for a private audience of one, "is to lend silence form."

PART ONE

THE SUCCESSFUL JOURNAL:
Practical Inspiration

It's very strange, but the mere act of writing anything is a help. It seems to speed one on one's way.

—KATHERINE MANSFIELD

CHAPTER I

Starting Out: Getting Lost on Purpose

∽

Once I begin the act of writing, it all falls away — the view from the window, the tools, the talismans, and I am unconscious of myself . . . one's carping inner critics are silenced for a time . . . there is always a surprise, a revelation. During the act of writing, I have told myself something that I didn't know I knew.

— GAIL GODWIN

JOURNALS. THEY BECKON everywhere. Stacked in neat rows in drugstores, fanned in pale rainbow hues in display windows, pyramided in bins at Wal-Mart, stocked near cash registers in bookstores. On corners of almost every major city, specialty journal shops have popped up overnight, as quickly and inevitably as Starbucks.

And at midnight in a speck of a prairie town, someone can order dozens from catalogs. A single click on the Internet connects another country — France for hand-made diaries, Italy for paper the color of fresh cream. Staring at the electronic images, a browser tries imagining a journal's weight in their hand.

But consider the most familiar, those from the local stationery store. Yesterday I went into mine and was instantly struck by the clean, dry smell of paper, the comforting sight of pens arrayed by colors. Stationery stores are the kingdom of childhood enjoyed in adulthood. The aisles brim with all that possibility, as if a 79¢ pen or a different type of notebook will do the trick this time. New pen, new paper, new self. Journals, once contained on a single shelf, now take over whole sections of stationery stores. I'm fascinated by the sheer range of them: blank or lined hardcover journals, their covers decorated with pale half-moons or tulips or ancient maps. Stacks of spiral notebooks marbleized like brain synapses. Others, so satisfying to the touch, are covered in canvas or burlap; a few are leather bound, discreet as expensive new shoes. From the practical to the private, they divide up a life — monthly, yearly, five-year diaries. Travel diaries. Nature journals. Children's first journals with covers the color of tangerines.

Nearby, stacks of legal pads wait to be inserted into black vinyl covers.

Ten million blank journals are sold annually in stationery stores alone. Two million in specialty stores. Thanks to secret passwords and specialized software, an estimated four million scribblers keep some form of journal on a computer. If the information age has spawned a hunger for connection (and privacy), so, too, a need for the quickest way to access interior life. Web sites pop up daily. Our accelerated global age has left little time to slow down and reflect. In Japan, for example, those too busy to keep journals phone in their entries. At the end of the month, a company sends a bound transcript.

Familiar with the statistics, I also know how hard it is for many to keep journals. Yet when I ask people, as I often do, who they wish *had* kept a diary, a torrent of names is unleashed — my mother, my husband, my sister, the uncle whom I'm named after, the father I never knew. Why then the resistance to keeping them ourselves? Virginia Woolf put her finger on it best perhaps, when she asked her own diary: "Whom do I tell when I tell a blank page?" Whom does one write for? Oneself, of course. "True to oneself — which self?" asked Woolf's friend and archrival, Katherine Mansfield. (In her journal, she confessed that a single day's "thousands of selves" made her feel like a hotel clerk busy handing keys to the psyche's "willful guests.")

Watching someone pause in a stationery store, journal in hand, I can almost hear the internal voices chattering away. The same annoying voices that distract the moment a journal's purchased or opened to the first page. *Why should I feel I have anything interesting to say? Isn't this a blabbing, confessional culture? Why add to it? What makes me so sure I'll keep up a journal this time? What if someone else* finds *it?*

I'm always tempted to tap the hesitant on the shoulder. I'd say that I wish I'd kept journals more minutely. Better, longer records: the exact way sunlight fell in dusty slants on floors in childhood; the smell of lemon and bacon in the morning; the startling dare of a first kiss. (Like others, though, I often placed a journal back on the store shelf, sure I'd remember everything.) I'd warn how others I've met, their voices full of sudden urgency, say they never understood the importance of journals until theirs were lost or stolen. Or describe how, safe on a shelf, journals proved invaluable when starting longer projects, like a memoir or family chronicle. I'd cite a single entry from a diary someone lent me: On January 12, 1879, a woman whose family had crossed and recrossed the western frontier wrote, "I would like to write a journal that my children could own and be benefitted by if I were taken away. If I were to leave them now, what would they ever know about me?" Thanks to that journal, five generations later a huge family is now linked.

The seasoned journal keeper, of course, doesn't need to be persuaded. It's a habit as natural and expansive as breathing. "Two and a half decades later," says novelist Gail Godwin, "my diary and I have an old marriage. The space between us is gone. I hardly *see* my diary anymore. And yet, there is a confident sense that we are working together." But hearing how effortless that is for others is like knowing someone who always finds a parking space with time already on the meter. Some trick or lucky gene that makes some able to keep journals, others not. But for most people, their resistance to journals is as strong as their attraction. The following are some reasons behind that resistance and ways to overcome it.

Why Write?: Myths and Mazes

That vast group. I can't forget those faces. Or the mass of hands that shoot up when I ask who has a hard time even *beginning* a journal.

27

Journals, more than any other form of self-expression, are invisibly weighted with false preconceptions. (Including the most obvious. "I never keep journals," I hear over and over, only to discover that people do, but just not in a form they recognize.) For many, journals seem to come with operating instructions: all those invisible *shoulds*. You know them by heart: a diary should be kept daily, in longhand, only in hardcover notebooks, never crossing out, always in full sentences.

The most commonly asked question new chroniclers ask is, *What's the difference between a diary and a journal?* A diary, traditionally, is thought of as a daily factual record; a journal, something kept more fitfully and for deeper reflection. A diary is *what I did* today; a journal *what I felt* about today. Yet it's not so simple (or boring) as that. May Sarton, who began her still bestselling *Journal of a Solitude* at sixty, wrote daily yet called her diaries journals. Thoreau, who wrote two million words in twenty-nine notebooks, kept both factual and meditative accounts in a single journal. Virginia Woolf, who used hers as a writer's sketchbook, called her journals diaries. Here's a helpful heresy: call them both. Use the words interchangeably. What does it matter as long as either does what it's supposed to: allows you, as Woolf said, to net "this loose, drifting material of life."

Both words come from the Latin root for day. A fancy fact, but here's its simpler truth: a diary or journal isn't necessarily something that should be *done* daily so much as it is a clue to how *to see the daily world* around oneself differently.

More diaries have been killed by the idea that a diary must be written in daily than by any other single thing. Why? It feels like homework. (What's worse, *you* assigned it, making the guilt even stronger when you take days, even months, off.) For many, it triggers early memories of that first unsuccessful diary. Literary agent Sally Brady started her first journal when, at eight, she was "taken out of school for two months to drive from Massachusetts to California and back. I had to keep a log every day, mother's orders. I'd write the date and then 'I hate this log.' At nine, my grandmother gave me a fat, red leather five-year diary, five lines per day, impossible to say much in. All those *accusing empty spaces.*"

While it's helpful for some to keep a daily log, most quickly get bored by recording just bare-bones facts. The trick is to spark them to life. It's best to start with realistic expectations, writing two to three times a week, alternating where and when you write. The exercises and journal prompts that follow at the end of each chapter will help. They're designed to jump-start you, get the writing out, generating material quickly so there's already a foundation.

Journals allow one to reflect, to step outside oneself. They create a third space, an invaluable pause between the conscious and unconscious self. Above all, journals are a way to let the world be reconsidered, not taking in the habitual. They're a master switch on tracks, moving us from the familiar, from not seeing, to seeing anew.

Getting Lost on Purpose

In "A Stranger's Way of Looking," poet Heather McHugh notes that a writer is "someone who has to get away in order to see what he was part of." The same is true for the journal keeper. "Each time we sit down to write," observes novelist Maria Flook, "we are leaving our homeport, our shoreline. We are getting ourselves lost on purpose." That, too, is one of the best ways of thinking about beginning a journal.

Getting lost on purpose is something our fast-paced, overscheduled lives rarely allow us to do. Those huge journal statistics hint at the hunger to do just that. It's behind the reason that *journal* has become a verb. At first it's enough just to record surface facts. Yet the moment they're put on the page, a deeper movement of the mind is set in motion. As any seasoned journal keeper will attest, one quickly learns to trust that a different, more supple kind of intelligence or memory bank is being tapped.

But why write? What's at stake? Like others who shared their stories, novelist Elizabeth Berg told me how vivid the memory still is of her first diary. In eighth grade she was given "a white diary with gold trim, and that all-important extra: a *lock*. Of course, I lost the key soon after I got the diary and had to cut it open. Then I Scotch-taped it shut and wrote KEEP OUT! in black Magic Marker — high security." Yet at age fifteen, "I remember it was summer, dusk, and I was at my Aunt Tish's house in Minnesota, getting ready for a party that my cousin was going to have that night. I was sitting at a dresser that had a big mirror, getting ready to do my makeup, and I all of the sudden looked at myself and thought, *Who* am *I?* I began to write the answer to that question on notebook paper, and I kept what I wrote, because it seemed important to me. It seemed like the truth. After that, I began keeping most of my writing — that kind of writing, anyway — in a black plastic notebook that I still have."

Often I ask others, "Who are we *really* writing for?" A future self, usually. Journal keeping is that rare activity centered in the present, contemplating the past, yet

31

aimed for a future self. But writing about oneself is often an obstacle for many. *Too selfish. Too self-absorbed.* (Was that number one or two on your why-I-can't-keep-a-journal list?) That punitive attitude is best captured by Jessica Mitford. Growing up in England, Mitford was sternly taken in hand by her nanny before any social occasion. "You're the least important person in the room," the nanny hissed, "and don't forget it." (Luckily, the future writer used her invisibility to observe, training her eye instead. Remembering. Recording.) The nanny's message, played out, gets internalized, of course, as our Censor, whose multiple guises have plagued writers for centuries.

Why Start a Journal

Unfortunately, the nanny didn't know the secret history of diaries. In seventeenth-century England, Quakers kept them as records of conscience. Writing daily about the self was seen as a way to *transcend* it. Early Quaker diaries stressed spiritual confession and gratitude. As journals gained popularity, the daily world crept in. (Think of Samuel Pepys writing so brilliantly on the great fire and plague in London in 1665–66.) Over the centuries, self-examination took a new step forward. Journals became the private place where the public mask could drop. And with it, journals themselves became an important way to suspend self-judgment. Today, sitting for even five minutes with a journal offers a rare cease-fire in the battle of daily life, a time when we're not graded, not performing. It's a time when one attempts some truth, silencing those carping inner voices.

At their core, journals are about sharpening consciousness, not stoking egotism. Trust that the bore bending your ear on a plane or the ranting taxi driver on the ride home never keeps a journal. Their egotism leaks out publicly instead. *You* become their journal, a live blank page held hostage in a seat. Think of journals as a safe, private way to have it siphoned off, rethought, vented. (Even the health value is high. According to findings published in the *Journal of the American Medical Association,* such writing alleviated the symptoms of patients with asthma and rheumatoid arthritis.) The deeper benefit of keeping a journal is that it offers a way to be consistently aware or mindful. As Katherine Mansfield noted, her journal became a way "to lose all that is superficial and acquired in me and to become a conscious, direct human being."

Journal writing is, foremost, a way to order and reframe perspective. For Samantha Harvey, an American who interrupted studies at Cambridge University to compete in the Olympics, "keeping a diary means living deliberately. The diary helps me weigh thoughts and opinions about life. And yet the final 'meaning' of everyday events remains open-ended, since the writing and evaluating is continually evolving. For me, the diary is the outward expression of this inward quest — to understand my relationship to myself, to others, to the world, to the spiritual. Without the diary process, it would be difficult to make sense of all the impressions of day-to-day life. Each night when I sit down to write, on a tiny scale, I'm making coherence out of the chaos."

Journals offer invaluable clues at every stage of a recorded life. For Katya Sabaroff Taylor, who's kept journals since childhood, "keeping a journal over a life-time has taught me a sense of compassion about the human condition, including my own." For ten-year-old Jessica Weaver, journals are where "I first heard my *real* voice, not the one already trying to please in school." For recent college graduate Arianne Miller, they are "a way to map and track decision-making in my life." For Ray Zager, a retired lawyer, "almost every part of me is in my diaries. My thoughts, dreams, awakenings, holding of the pen (as taught by my third-grade teacher), reading and writing, power and exercise of auditory skills. Other memory is empowered as well. Friends push their way into its pages." For Julie Houy, "I am eighty-one. It helps me to age well."

Most beginning journals are a jumble, an eclectic inventory, the patterns yet to be linked. Yet they're there. A diarist in her late twenties notes, "My journals have taken the form of discovering the undiscovered, a biographical sketch of my shadow self." To begin a diary is like a detective search, a natural activity for anyone who's ever loved reading a mystery, or tackled the simplest crossword puzzle. "Writing in a journal," a woman in her late sixties says, "has always been a way to gather up what I felt were the fragments of my life, a sort of follow-the-dots connection that ends up with a full-blown sketch of life, leaving behind a record for my children."

The Forms a Journal Can Take: A Capacious Holdall

Like me when I was in my twenties, you can know why and even for whom you're keeping a journal and still be hobbled by the sheer mechanics.

Often people think that a diary should look like, well, a diary: a classic bound journal usually. Or something easily identified as a prop in a movie: a hardcover journal with a quill pen.

A journal is anything that's begun to be committed to paper and saved. A journal is as much *an intention to record and save* as it is a physical form. My own journals, depending on their purpose, range from Italian-made notebooks to files stuffed with paper to cheap spiral notebooks. The forms journals take are as idiosyncratic and varied as the millions who keep them. Among the ways: Several years' worth of the same 89¢ stenographer's pads. Filled-in pages of calendar squares saved yearly in accordion files. Computer disks. Three-ring binders. Scraps of paper kept in a shoebox. Legal pads. Joint e-mails printed out and saved. The same notebook lined up on windowsills: tiny spiral notebooks from Barnes and Noble, recyclable paper covers. Composition notebooks with black-and-white speckled fronts. Blue 5 x 7 cloth-bound artist's sketch books.

Some of the most successful diarists often use unconventional forms. Thoreau tore off birch bark as he walked around Walden Pond, jotting down ideas with pencils he'd made himself. Novelist Ron Carlson once stored scraps of paper in an old bag, now in computer files. One diarist I know finally got going by razoring out the few pages he'd managed to keep in a series of abandoned journals, transcribing them onto his computer. After a stroke, May Sarton was forced to dictate into a tape recorder. This, too, became a journal.

Woolf's metaphor of diary as a "deep old desk, a capacious hold-all," is also a license to use one's creative imagination, inventing forms. A diary should feel as comfortable as those worn slippers you refuse to throw out. Whatever its evolving form, it should help conjure up the feeling Elizabeth Berg describes when she thinks of her journals: "How wonderful they feel in the hand, how you can sit in a chair with your legs tucked under you and use a nice fountain pen to just quietly scratch away. No plugs, no keyboard, no screen. You write under a yellow lamplight, of course. A ticking clock nearby. And a dog at your feet, sleeping and whining out his nose when he comes to the good part of his dream. And, oh, it's winter, snowing."

The Well-Lived Examined Life

"The unrecorded life," Emerson observed, "is not worth examining." For many, though, the final, most stubborn lament is, When I try keeping a journal, mine are always boring, self-conscious, hard.

Consider the case of Jim Cummings, who, starting at thirteen, hasn't missed recording a day in forty-eight years. "To me, a diary is a record of verification. It is a proof that one has lived and that one has cared enough about a precious life to describe it." Keeping a diary makes him want to *lead* an interesting life, so he can record an interesting one. And he's done just that. In addition to keeping what's considered the longest continuous English-language diary, he has sixteen thousand diaries written by others that he stores in a special room in his Wisconsin shop. Since 1958, when he was just out of the army, he's earned a living as a bookseller specializing in published diaries of so-called ordinary lives. Shelf after shelf teems with journals, many of them centuries old. Among them are also rare ones kept by children, pioneer women, Civil War soldiers, gold rush miners, war prisoners.

He counts seven generations of journal keepers within his own family. "It's almost a genetic compulsion to keep diaries, like salmon spawning." His truck driver father, for example, kept nature and travel journals from 1933 to 1994, which have been purchased by the Minnesota Historical Society. Cummings's own diaries and collection are being sought by numerous historical and university libraries willing to offer $2 million to become the permanent site.

"A journal-keeper is really the natural historian of his own life," observes writer Verlyn Klinkenborg. "But many of the great journals," he notes, "are marked by a dogged absence of self-consciousness, a willingness to suspend judgment of the journal itself." Diaries, in the end, are about making connections. About getting around your unconscious mind. About breaking into your own store of preserved memories, stories, projects. About stealing them back to the light of day. To keep a journal is to learn how to play. Deeply. Even when a page is recording hard, impossible things, if judgment is suspended, there's always a surprise or shift. Connections made over time suddenly link, opening and transforming.

Freedom, play, insights, connections. These are what happen when a journal is defined on your own terms.

Released of the "should"s, even choosing a journal that feels right is a creative act. "In my closet there is a shelf entirely devoted to notebooks," says novelist Mary Gordon. "I buy notebooks wherever I go in the world. Just as each country has a different cuisine, each has a different notebook culture. And friends who know my fetish bring me notebooks from their travels." I love buying handmade Italian journals with pastel marbled covers. Often, though, they sit orphaned on my shelves. Their formality can make me too self-conscious, the task of writing too monumental. (I have terrible handwriting. It feels a crime to mar such perfect paper.) So I give them to friends who'd never write in anything but them.

British-born Kathleen Hornby has settled on just such notebooks for "ideas, inspirations useful to writing, quotations from famous writers, anything that pertains to books." For her and others, choosing a notebook is a ritual with rules as subtly complex as a Japanese tea ceremony. "Why do I put so much importance on the color of the cover, the feel of the paper, the very heft of such a humble object? Why can't I resist buying yet another one simply because I liked how it looked?" Because, she notes, it promises to "spark me." The paper is "silky to the touch, making it possible to believe I'm writing effortless prose as the pen on paper is so fluid, unobtrusive, even silent. I have a pile of notebooks on my desk, used and unused. They're like old, soft cardigans, comforting to have around, to pull on when the breeze blows."

Whatever physical form a journal takes, Italian handmade or deposit slips thrown in a shoe box, here are a few voices on what a diary truly is:

"A blank-faced confidante."

"Shelter."

"My memory's memory."

"A hidden savings account."

"Where all my creative work first hides."

"Life's rough draft I can edit."

"A way to travel while sitting perfectly still."

And, finally, Gertrude Stein, ever to the point: "A diary means yes indeed."

EXERCISES AND JOURNAL PROMPTS

- Off the top of your head, list all the forms, physical or otherwise, you can now imagine a journal taking. The wilder, often the better.

- On a sheet of loose-leaf paper, recall your very first diary. To start, simply jot details in sentence fragments. Divide the page into sections with the following heads: *What did it look like?* ("black cowhide cover, blank pages"; "a three-year white leather diary with a cunning little gold key I wore around my neck"; "red spiral-bound college notebook"; "a cheap drugstore diary with a Renoir on the cover.") *When did you get it?* ("8th-grade birthday gift — the most interesting thing truly *is* what I had for dinner each night.") *Why?* ("At 7, I was always telling stories. My great-grandmother gave me a book with blank pages"; "At 26, I went to France. I wrote down all I took in so I would still feel like I was sharing my life with my then-boyfriend"; "At 64, I bought one as a graduation gift for a niece and decided to keep her company.") *What single good thing did it spark?* ("My grandmother Baba sent me my first diary for my 13th birthday," writes Katya Taylor, "just when I needed it most: after the breakup of my first teenage romance, my parakeet, Keeto, was killed by my cat, and Baba was to die of lung cancer. But more than 40 years later I still keep a journal. It gave me a spiritual connection to my grandmother that continues to this day.") *If you stopped, what did you most miss?* ("My life.")

∽ A premise and working technique throughout this book is using the flip side of a notebook page (or even a receipt) to catch the ways we split thoughts. Think of it as: Received Opinions; New Perceptions. Use one side to record, the flip side to comment on. (Ideally, one side is lined, the other blank.) Take a moment now before continuing, to jot your most deeply held beliefs about journal keeping; use the other side to explore which beliefs ring untrue, are inherited, or blindly accepted.

CHAPTER II

Triggering Memory

The journal is the ideal place of refuge for the inner self because it constitutes a counterworld: a world to balance the other.

— JOYCE CAROL OATES

A WOMAN DRESSED in sheer white summer muslin sits at a writing desk, hand on notebook. Her suitor, interested in it and her, stands nearby. "Do you really keep a diary?" he asks. "I'd give anything to look at it. May I?" Smiling, the woman covers the page. "Oh, no," she replies. "You see, it is simply a very young girl's record of her own thoughts and impressions, and consequently meant for publication. When it appears in volume form I hope you will order a copy."

In this famous scene from his play *The Importance of Being Earnest,* Oscar Wilde scored a hit. In 1895, when it premiered, audiences laughed in recognition. They still do. Wilde mocks the cliché of the self-conscious diary keeper with his own twist — a private diary *meant* for public eyes. The scene rings true for other reasons: our image of writing in a journal, the necessity of privacy, our fear that someone might read it, and, secretly, the hope that a diary will be the start of significant work.

Wilde's serene Cecily is the idealized image that even seasoned journal keepers confess haunts them, slowing them down. Perri Klass, a novelist, pediatrician, and mother of three, evokes it: "In my mind is an image of the perfect diarist. Pensive, ruminative, leisurely, sitting in a cozy bookish room, filling a leather-bound notebook with even, clear writing, musing without self-consciousness." It's "everything mine are not."

Or mine. Or most people's. Four notebooks, 1989–94, are open as I write this. None match. Yet when I look at their covers, here's what I see: how I learned to keep a journal successfully. These are the notebooks with the lists. The blueprints.

The secret of keeping a journal is seeing it as a draft, a stepping-stone, a process. When I scribble in a notebook, I think of those dime-store tablets I had as a kid on which you'd draw and then lift the gray sheet, magically erasing the lines. Each time I flip to the reverse side of a page or write the next entry in a different colored ink, I lift the gray sheet. It took years of keeping journals to trust a simple fact: like life in transit, the writing inside is often fragmented, messy.

Journals are a process first. In time, they're process *and* product. "Some friends were over for lunch," recalls retired teacher Lisa Colt. "We talked about being either process or product people. I feel myself the former. And yet the physical product of all those tattered journals in the laundry room reminds me that I do have something to show. My journals remind me of the many short stops on a pilgrimage, or one woman's travels through a labryinth."

Moving Out of the Labryinth: Censorship, Privacy, and Secrecy

At the start, even getting past a second page can reveal a kind of labyrinth. "I feel so guilty," one woman told me. "There's this horrible irony. Journals are about freeing up the mind, but often magnify my self-consciousness." Scratch the surface and three culprits always emerge: the internal Censor (and maddening companions); the necessity for privacy; the security of secrecy. A moment on each. To control these three fears is to unlock the secret of how to slip under the surface of the conscious mind where connections — and freedom — flourish.

It's estimated that sixty-five thousand thoughts float through our mind a day. I don't know about you, but my internal voices comment on, veto, and squabble over about sixty-four thousand of them. That's on a good day. Journals sort. They wait till we're ready to cool or confirm stored impressions. In time, journals silence the sabotaging voices — the Censor, the procrastinator, the perfectionist. Those rob not only true voice, but confidence itself. A *New Yorker* cartoon shows a man at his desk. "Dear Diary," he writes. "Sorry to disturb you again."

Censoring the Censor

The Censor. It's that tight muscle of perfectionism. That dark, icy whisper. That confidence thief. I've never met a person who didn't believe theirs was the most demanding on the planet.

Mine is. Or was. Before I began keeping journals, I agreed with Thomas Mann that "a writer is someone for whom writing is more difficult than it is for other people." This was inconvenient, for my first job was as a writer. Starting out as a literary journalist before moving on to a career as a freelance writer, I read biographies for practical inspiration. I then put together an interview series called "Writers and Their Inspiration" in which I would quiz famous poets and novelists about their work habits. Inspired by a friend who's cheered up by keeping a file of clippings on catastrophes, natural and man-made, I kept a journal on how others over the centuries outfoxed their Censor. I stumbled on the formula instinctively: humor, determination, and serious play. I offer a range of quirky solutions to pull from a bag of tricks.

It's your life, your rules. Invent rules to suit you. Here are a sampling of highly idiosyncratic habits: Before computers, Saul Bellow used two typewriters: one for fiction, one for nonfiction. Balzac wrote in a white monk's robe, a pair of gold scissors (for editing?) suspended around his neck. Truman Capote preferred working in others' homes. But he wouldn't "tolerate the presence of yellow roses — which is sad because they're my favorite flower. I can't allow three cigarette butts in the ashtray. . . . Won't begin or end anything on a Friday."

At least twice a week, write in a different place. John Updike has four rooms in his house, each for a different type of writing (fiction, nonfiction, essays, letters), each with its own writing instrument (computer, legal pads, loose-leaf paper). He just goes from room to room whenever he's stuck. Journals, ever portable, make this trick a snap. Isaac Bashevis Singer, whom I interviewed just before he won the Nobel Prize in Literature, limbered up by making notes first in a coffee shop near his apartment. (I thought he was wearing a suit and tie for the interview. He wore them daily, I learned, to intimidate his Censor.)

Catch the Censor off guard. Write at odd moments in even odder spots. This week I filled pages: while waiting for gas — full tank and oil check — (cheap spiral notebook kept in my handbag); while stuck on hold (index cards near the phone); in a grocery line (back of bank deposit slips).

Let the Censor think you're not doing anything. Connections come fast and furious when the stakes are low. While I later copy many things into permanent notebooks, I save old envelopes to jot on. In a kind of shell game, Mary Mitchell changes her notebooks often. They've ranged from "a pink autograph book; supermarket receipts; a corduroy pocket-size blank book; fancy leather journals; a memo pad in her purse; composition books." Using cheap pads, another diarist notes, "is like living in a cottage as opposed to a stately home. By keeping it small, I avoid setting large expectations for myself. That way I'm able to live up to them." Freedom allows play, which allows creativity. Brahms spent years perfecting a shrine to his favorite composers; he composed only in the small bare room off it.

Give the Censor a voice. Expose the nonsense. Like a vampire, the voice withers in direct light. Transcribe the whispers. It will read like a bizarre ticker tape. Something like this: stupid, stupid, wrong word, terrible, trite, who cares?, badly written, find another word, Bigger Word, write to impress, be quotable." The moment Kafka wrote in his journal, "Distractedness, weak memory, stupidity. Days passed in futility," it broke the grip of writer's block.

Write the Censor a letter. It's a deceptively simple trick that yields dramatic effects. Gail Godwin calls her combination procrastinator-perfectionist the Watcher, who rejects thoughts too soon, constantly interrupting. Tired of being urged to drop writing and drive to the library "to check on the name of a flower or a World War II battle," she finally wrote him a letter. It helped free her.

Kill or at the very least fire the Censor. (I tend to favor homicide.) The creativity the Censor stifles quickly rises to the surface in this simple exercise. I've seen it done as a bullet-ridden murder mystery; an all-dialogue jury trial; a log of a week being tormented. To show me how severe her Censor was, someone singed the edges of the exercise. Two now-successful journal keepers used the following entries to confront their Censor. They keep them pasted in the front of a journal:

You smell of dried fish, bony and crisp. When did you arrive? Were you carrying that bottomless brown suitcase of erasers, razor blades, and blank pages? Did I stand with arms open, or eyes shut? Was I thirteen? Ten? Five? I remember how smoothly you unpacked, settling in, as if you were returning home from a long journey. Even now there are days when you are quiet, emerging only after I write, saying, "Burn it. Erase it. Purge the words choking your life. They are worthless, no one will like them, no one will love you. Come on, throw them away."

And

Writing throws me into uncertainty and fear. I seek control and escape. If someone asks a Spaniard for directions, he'll give them and then add, "And if you don't find your destination, nothing bad will happen." But I am not in Spain. I am writing at my desk Even as I write this, I'm wondering if I'm doing it right. The voice says, "Don't risk. Don't include this. It doesn't fit. It should all fit together like a visual puzzle."

The Censor, fat as a tick with pride, hates not being taken seriously. Humor is the sharpest weapon. Whenever his internal voices make him self-conscious, a man I know transcribes them immediately — but as the Marx brothers. One diarist, parodying how the rules left over from high school creep into a journal, wrote: "I (no, not I, never use I) . . . Well, (Don't use that either! Too casual. I have to impress with big words.)"

The Compass Point Reads: Forward, Forward

You're *not* the only one with these voices homesteading in your brain. Da Vinci, a terrible perfectionist, kept journals for forty years as a way to generate work and outwit his Censor. In the morning, he recorded his dreams. In the afternoon, he jotted notes for ideas. In the evening, he recorded passages from his reading. He did each with lightning speed, his goal solely to map out as many ideas as possible before his Censor could veto them.

From one of my old notebooks, always worth remembering:

Don't let the pen lift from the page. Write a page

without stopping. Write another. On the next, start the page in the center and write in a spiral. Watch the Censor's voice spiral like a dark cyclone. "I'd been brutally intolerant of keeping a diary," a woman told me, "until I saw that spiral with all my Censor's hidden rules: wait — write only when inspired; be profound or don't bother. Now I catch myself writing on month-old brochures with drying pens."

Write fast. Do whatever promotes speed so the hand works faster than the carping voices. For most people, it's easiest writing in longhand. A wife notes: "I've grown used to my scrawl and hardly flinch because longhand has its own rhythms that soothe *and* stimulate." Her husband says, "My brain doesn't flow into my fingers as well as typing into a computer." Others swear by time-honored tools: "Pilot extrafine pens," "Schaffer fountain pens (I love the flow of the ink — it lends itself to a calligraphic kind of script — but when desperate will write with anything)."

Make the strange familiar, the familiar strange. Write at a slant. M. Elaine Mar, who moved from Chinese calligraphy as a child to journals in English before publishing a memoir, still often writes upside down to trick the Censor. Others I know write a page with a nondominant hand or with eyes closed. Some doodle first. Or use different-colored paper every other time.

Diamonds of the Dustheap

The subtlest journal habits I take from Virginia Woolf. Walk before writing. The mind limbers along with the legs. Catch the brain off guard: write when *tired*. Write in fragments. A journal propped on her knee at tea, Woolf wrote without lifting the pen, not stopping for spelling, grammar, or punctuation. "If it were not written faster than the fastest typewriting, if I stopped and took thought, it would never be written at all," she wrote. The mind, she knew, is triggered by quick, loose associations. "The advantage," she told her diary, "is that it sweeps up accidentally several stray matters which I should exclude if I hesitated, which are the diamonds of the dustheap."

The twenty-first-century solution: turn down the brightness light on the computer. Freewrite. The Censor can't see what you're writing. Print out, underline what's good, copy that into a journal as a way to get started.

Getting Going, Staying Going

As a child, I wrote the date, then: "Nothing." But the few times I began with the other clichéd diary opening — a sentence describing the weather — something odd happened. I wrote. Often what got triggered was a surprise, an unexpected connection. For centuries, diarists have noted date or weather, not for accuracy but as an icebreaker. At the start, the hand and mind work together, stretching, limbering, relaxing into what waits to be discovered under the surface.

Here are some ways I've discovered to get beneath the surface. Copying out someone's words quickly triggers your own. "I repeatedly write one line until the engine is going," says a college student. "I copy lyrics into my journal. Usually the singer has said what I am feeling better than I ever could." I often jump-start myself with a quote. (I keep a list in a special notebook.) My favorites work on a paradox, giving the mind a bone to chew on. Recently, I copied two riddles into a notebook from the Greek philosopher Heraclitus: "Expect the unexpected or you won't find it, because it doesn't leave a trail," and "A wonderful harmony arrives from joining together the seemingly unconnected."

Or start with seed phrases: "If only"; "I always must remember"; "You said"; "Imagine." One diarist I met writes "the alphabet in journal margins, one letter each line. Then, without thinking, I come up with as many words beginning with the letter. The strange pairings always triggers me." Get rid of words altogether. Joan

Miller, an artist and art teacher, has kept journals for fifty-three years. "I do mind-mapping first — spider legs of ideas flowing from a central circle. Some aspect of my life in the middle with people, places, influences at each leg."

Privacy: Other Voices, Other Rooms

My grandmother's Siberian journal, I now see, was a form of mapping a life. It was also a way to hide in plain sight. It showed her confident in her Red Cross surgical scrubs, for example, but never told the hidden story that she'd joined up partly to escape poverty. Having to wear a uniform daily was convenient when you couldn't afford new clothes. In her visual journal that committed nothing in writing, she safely pasted in photos instead. To stare at endless photos of her smiling, surrounded by that temporary family of medical colleagues, is almost to forget the lonely orphanage years she never recorded in any diary.

The fear someone might read a diary is the Censor's lazy trump card. You self-censor instead. Privacy is key. In the icy information age where the click of a key prints out a life's facts for strangers' eyes, a journal is a rare place of privacy. "It's very important that no one read my journal but me," says Elizabeth Berg. "You need a mirror where you can stick your stomach out *all* the way."

No matter what else they record, journals are often solace simply because they are private. Anger flares and cools on the same page. Lies get untwisted; truths told. And then one links back to the world. Stumbling on my mother's journal as a child, I knew she wouldn't have hidden it in the linen closet if I was meant to read it. So I didn't. Alice James uncorked her psyche's "bottled lightning," writing privately about a "geyser of emotions, sensations, speculations and reflections." Neither of her famous brothers — novelist Henry, philosopher William — knew about the diary until after her death. (Dying, she dictated the final pages to her closest friend, who kept the journal secret for two years.) Anne Frank slipped her diary into her father's briefcase every night. A hidden diary in a locked briefcase in the Secret Annex.

Over the centuries, diarists have gone to great lengths to ensure privacy. For a millennium in the western region of China's Hunan province, women have written in Nushu, a secret diary language known only to them. Da Vinci kept his journals in handwriting decipherable only when held up to a mirror. Samuel Pepys kept his in code. Anaïs Nin kept a "decoy" diary for her husband, erecting a false closet wall for the originals. Tired of wearing a gold key around her neck for each current diary, she deposited them in a bank vault. (Nin, though, had a lot to hide, including husbands on both coasts.)

Diary keeping taps a sense of safety often missing in childhood. Robert Pfaff, the son of a conservationist, grew up in a house that included hummingbirds, falcons, a screech owl named Picasso, baby opossums "that hung from your fingertips and smelled like puppies." As a child, he watched his mother heal the exotic, including a baby sperm whale. He wrote about that world, moving from journals to memoir in my class at Harvard. He says:

"As a child I craved privacy. In our house, so filled with the living, there was no room for solitude and reflection. My brother and I shared a bedroom, and my mother despised our locking the door. I built secret hideouts in the woods, found clearings under bushes, dug tunnels in the marsh, where I could create my own world. I once bought a book on dinosaurs and wrote DO NOT DISTURB across the front, as if on a door, as if the words and pictures inhabited a living world. The book wasn't another toy. It was somewhere.

"Around ten, I bought my first diary. Blue faux leather, with the word *Diary* in gold letters across the cover. A broad lock with two keys. My new diary held all the power of heresy, an act of rebellion. A gift for myself, something I savored and feared. To this day, I believe this explains my poor handwriting. That raw energy of self-revelation coming through the pen, making thoughts visible, declaring oneself.

"Like the dinosaur book, the journal became another space. I'd store my secrets inside. I'd crawl inside and live there. I buried one key in the backyard in a glass jar. The other I wore around my wrist. Then one day I wrote only one sentence across the title page: I think I am gay.

"I closed the diary, tugged on the lock, and buried it under the carpet under the chest of drawers in our bedroom closet. After that, I never wrote anything else in that childhood diary. My diary sat there for months — until, in fear of its being discovered, I tore out the title page and threw it in the garbage."

Secrecy: Hidden in Plain Sight

"I must be private, secret, as anonymous and submerged as possible in order to write," Virginia Woolf confided to her diary. Across London, Katherine Mansfield wrote in hers, "One tries to go deep — to speak to a secret self we all have." "I know that, come what may, you always keep a secret," Anne Frank wrote in her diary. Journals are where in secrecy we first find the voice that will carry us through the world.

Sometimes that voice is urged out a bit too early. "It started for me," remembers writer Patricia Hampl, "with one of those red leatherette five-year diaries, bolted shut by a diminutive brass lock whose ineffectual key I hid elaborately in my bedroom. A journal not only required secrecy — it was secrecy." But one day "my brother, idly curious, didn't even bother to search for the little key; he coolly sprang the lock with a bent paper clip, and laughed himself silly. My first reader."

The world is full of moral sneaks: siblings, parents, roommates, spouses. Spies in the house of love or work. "Well, I hope your life isn't *really* as interesting as your diary!" a father blurted to his teenage daughter. A woman I know in the middle of a bitter divorce had her diaries subpoenaed. The ploy backfired: the entries only confirmed she wanted the marriage to work. The Texas jury was outraged by the woman's invasion of privacy. She won $1 million in additional settlement.

I polled my most recent memoir class: Where do you hide journals? Slips of paper came back like anonymous ballots.

"I write in a foreign language. I was a French major. It keeps my skills up, my kids out."

"I buy boring textbooks, cut the heart out, fit the diary inside. Who'll open *Probate Tax?*"

"In a toolbox. Luckily, my handwriting is also indecipherable."

"In a box of feminine napkins (jumbo size)."

"On my computer. Secret files. Secret passwords."

"On the open shelf. On each cover I've written, *Read at your own peril.*"

"By making a collage journal. Pasting in visual images from magazines. I create a kind of private code. Symbols of things I don't want others to read in a private journal."

"I write in public places for privacy. I write in slanted, mirror image to block conscious thought."

Soon I'll tell how individuals who had diaries lost or stolen turned it to their advantage, in some cases into published stories. But first, remember: each of the people I've mentioned in this chapter survived. Each began by finding a private space to write in. Each wrote in secrecy, hands covering a notebook. And as in the case of Wilde's resourceful Cecily, the diary became a doorway to other writing or projects.

And those who never keep journals, out of fear or self-censorship? The final twist of secrecy: lives hidden from themselves. Memories lost. "I just don't remember anymore," they say blankly to their children or grand-children. Lives leaving not a trace, just shadows.

EXERCISES AND JOURNAL PROMPTS

☞ On a sheet of paper, do a mind map. In the center write: Censor. Let each spider line be a person or event that, like Frankenstein's body parts, gave life to your Censor (third grade teacher; first boss; ex-spouse). Off that line do smaller ones that record what they said. In red pen, give a failing grade to each early Censor. Now that you've flunked them, reimagine the original scene. It's a way to lift the gray sheet.

☞ Over the course of a single day, write down the Censor's whispers on index cards. At the end of the day, throw them away.

CHAPTER III

Ways of Seeing: The Present-Tense World

∽

Memory is a living thing — it too is in transit. But during its moment, all that is remembered joins and lives — the old and the young, the past and the present, the living and the dead.

— EUDORA WELTY

YESTERDAY THE mail brought that secret astonishment, ever rarer in a speedy era: real letters. They're ones with wavy postmarks and stamps stuck on crookedly in haste, but by hand. All this last year they've come, several a week. So have packages. Opening bulky mailers, I find excerpts from a dream journal, and the published scientific paper that first started in it; passages copied from a war journal; photocopied travel diaries; retyped entries written when someone was homeless; and a manual from a high school teacher near Berkeley who, tired of sluggish classes, invented his own journal software to motivate students. (My husband, tossing out the *To: Occupant* flyers, is astonished by this mail. How, he wonders, can such a private activity as journal keeping generate so many people willing to talk about journals? But by now he knows once a journal becomes part of a life, stories spark off it like a force field.)

I recognize one correspondent's handwriting at once. It has the same italic slant of the final entry she made in a journal I'd taken across country. At the time, I was on tour for my previous book. After the readings or workshops, I had anyone who was interested write a few words in the journal I had brought with me. At night, I'd then read this collective journal. Some said they liked knowing that it had been a gift from novelist Alice Hoffman, a favorite writer of many. Or that they were glad I, too, found writing in such a beautiful journal hard. Others had no problem writing in it. It's almost completely filled now with things others had to say on journals, including this by a woman in San Francisco: "In journals," she scribbled, "I have access to a kind of wisdom, some consistent sense of self, I don't ordinarily possess in fragmented daily life. Looking back I want to know who I really was, not some facsimile created and carried around in my current mind."

In yesterday's mail, she sent a twist on that story: "Years ago my elder daughter had my permission to read my high school diaries. Over six months, she read them again and again, asking many questions about my high school life. (She'd just started hers, those miserable teenage years.) Then we had a fight. She knew the best way to hurt me was to destroy the diaries. It was. An irreplaceable part of my life lost. So many of my photographs, writing and souvenirs. I wish I could have them back. But most of all, I spoke at that time with a voice I no longer have."

For her the years 1946–51 are gone. I know she's long since kept journals. She knows that a great deal of future writing will come out of them. But what to tell her about those lost journals? About how Hemingway's first wife lost the suitcase in which she'd carefully packed the draft of his first book? He said it was the best thing. Now he could rewrite it honestly. (Okay, this was Hemingway, what else do you think he'd say?) Or about how Mary Laub, who won the jury settlement after her 1984–95 diaries were paraded in court, kept on writing, including during trial breaks.

Life brims with creative thieves: Tolstoy found the kernel of *War and Peace,* including its heroine's name, in a story sketched in his future wife's diary. That famous daffodil poem, the bane of every schoolkid, seized Wordsworth's imagination as he read his sister's nature journal. (Dorothy openly shared it "to give William pleasure.") Critics hailed Raymond Radiguet's novel *Devil in the Flesh* only to learn, decades later, he'd stolen their favorite passages directly from his lover's diary. At the time, the diarists probably felt their lives — and journals — as boring as that thankless host of daffodils. Yet in another's eyes, a diary shimmers with concrete details, life patterns, a self unaware of its own stories.

So how to see a journal with fresh eyes from the start? How to unlock (or re-create) the archive of memory? The beginning diarist has an advantage here, but I hope seasoned journal keepers will consider seeing a journal from scratch. For this chapter, inspired by the story of those lost high school diaries, focuses on how to link memory and successful diary productivity.

Memory and Meaning: Finding the Image That Unlocks Them

Most diaries are abandoned out of boredom, not knowing what to write about, or fear that what's being recorded has no value. Pity the famous. Required by posterity to keep diaries, they cover these fears with facts. History's most famous diaries are notoriously unreflective. Queen Victoria's six decades of diaries (rewritten by her daughter) are an interminable litany of teas under hot colonial suns and drizzly English skies. Tsar Nicholas II, oblivious to the brewing Russian Revolution, noted cloud formations, subtle shifts in weather, pressure drops. As mobs stormed the Bastille, Louis XVI's diary for July 14, 1789, records only a single word, *"Rien!"* (Nothing!). Each was trapped by their idea of a journal as just a log of daily life.

A journal is how memory and meaning finally meet, finding a core image that begins to unlock important connections in a life. But to get there, consider five important practical suggestions woven throughout this book: suspend any notion of what a journal should look like or how often it should be written in; write as if to the one friend you'd never betray (it may be yourself, or, like Anne Frank, an ideal imagined reader); go between multiple journals to spur productivity; in time, give each new journal a specific purpose; play, letting each page be a process first, each entry like a Polaroid, easily taken, easily discarded, yet telling you what to do next.

All this comes together when you let a stray fact or single memory spark the true beginning. However you've kept journals till now, try a technique that begins with the present world but is designed to trigger memory and frame stories that emerge from it. Life is dense with details, ever-shifting versions of oneself. Journals seem simple: you start with your life. But where? Now? At birth? The wedding? Divorce? First day of retirement?

Finding or narrowing material stumps many. A simple warm-up exercise of making lists can dissolve that block. Lists limber the mind, focus its material, tap deep into the unconscious, finding its hidden interests. I often make them when I've got a cold. It clears the head immediately. Make three columns. In the first, randomly list ten separate years in your life. Next, ten places. Last, ten people. Without stopping to think, go across the columns, circling four key items in each category. Make columns from just those. Now select one in each column and put them in a final list. That's where you begin. In front of you is a master list, some code of memory, you've given yourself to decode. Trust your instincts. Your hand, like a magnet, simply found what I call the hot spots in the details. Write quickly to know why these three items won out.

The best way to start is by trying something I finally noticed I've long been doing in my own diaries:

writing tiny narrative snapshots, a paragraph to two pages. Triggered by a list, each wrote itself quickly. A saved museum stub I'd noted in a list, for example, sparked a sketch about a summer in Italy when I first met someone who lent me an apartment. In time, I noticed the chain: moving from writing about an object to a place to a single incident. The sketches became building blocks, an opening out, working as memory itself works — sparked by concrete or strong sensory details. The lists gave me triggers, kernels, seeds; the snapshots linked memory and meaning by showing me a rich array of stored — and therefore important — images.

Snapshot writing was a revelation, a constant source of inspiration. I stopped worrying about capturing today in anything but telegram-fast jottings. I began to see that writing from the cool shadowy recesses of memory was how to begin journals. I arrived at meaning through a series of guided accidents. The present was often best revealed by tapping the past, immediate or sometimes from childhood. (Anyone who fears resurrecting the miseries of childhood only has to read a single page of Frank McCourt's *Angela's Ashes* to see how pain is stored by the adult mind, and that joy is remembered and released when one is writing from the senses.)

Object Lessons

The summer I was eight I found myself stranded in an August arts workshop. While my brother rounded baseball diamonds, his foot tapping dust in magic puffs from canvas bags, I sat inside with other third-grade girls. The windows always seemed shut. The teacher, a wiry brunette, was permanently headachy. Waiting for the aspirin to kick in, she invented things for us to do quietly. Studying objects on a tray to improve memory was a success, as it's the only one I remember. I'd stare hard at the strange items she'd improvised, closing my eyes only to see them float in memory: a magnifying glass, an acorn, two house keys. On the way home, though, I found I kept thinking about the other items, how the gourd was like a pebbly brain, or the coins she'd scattered seemed small compared to the pile my father tossed nightly onto his bureau. (In those days, I thought what he emptied from his pocket was what he'd earned that day.)

Years later I saw the real lesson I learned in staring at that tray: objects are encoded with life stories. They brim with unexplored narrative. Objects remind us of all the things that should have been recorded in journals but never were. All day long we surround ourselves with objects that remind us who we or others are. Anything kept permanently on a desk, taken to college, hidden in a closet yet never to be parted with teems with stories. Just a glance triggers a world of associations — who we were with, when and where and why.

Such objects can be quick inspiration triggers. Begin with a single item, something that you've had at least six months. It may be as simple as a photo or cheap souvenir — or something that has no obvious value in another's eye: a saved theater stub, an odd-shaped rock. It may be an object stashed in a cupboard and only taken out occasionally, or the first thing you'd rescue in a fire. Use ten minutes to freewrite, jotting down precise details to describe what it looks like. How would you describe it to a stranger? Imagining another person helps you make the description concrete, countering the worst tendency in journals — their cloudy, complaining abstractions. Fill a page. Wait a day. Select four or five significant details and jot down why you chose this object. Then let your hand begin to tell the story it has long stored.

Images and stories will release in a rush. Look for the live wires, the incongruous, those slightly off-center details. They're the surest clues to where memory stores deeper meaning. They'll guide you to what you wanted to tell yourself. From journals I've seen: A diamond solitaire in a velvet ring box. One detail — a faint outline on the box's inner satin lining "faint as a water stain" — suggested the slow changes spreading in a marriage. A blue, plastic baby comb "thin as a wafer. If I rub my finger down the teeth, I hear a zipping sound." It evoked the strange travel day a baby was adopted. The feel of a silver mesh bracelet on skin conjured childhood visits to the museum to see the armor and the suppler, invisible armor now worn daily as a lawyer.

A violin remembered in midlife by Cynthia Thompson triggered a story closer to home. In her journal she jotted: "The violin smelled of old wood, sweat, and rosin. It resembled most others — a brown thick-waisted figure eight with baroque curves. Its surface — holes shaped like an 'S' in old script. Ebony fixtures: chin rest, tail piece and fingerboard, linked by metal strings in tension over a miniature suspension bridge." Four sentences in a journal summoned a series of unfurling memories: how a burglar in Philadelphia had stolen the violin she'd owned since childhood; how her father had taken her shopping, trying to find the tonal richness of that lost violin. The final memory was of her father replacing the lost violin.

The journal snapshot that evolved, though, led elsewhere. With the new violin, she and her father entered her mother's hospital room. Standing on the cold linoleum floor, Cynthia played Schubert. Once a gifted pianist and music teacher, her mother, in the final stages of illness, was soothed, listening to her favorite composer. As her mother listened, "her breathing through a valve in her neck grew harsh with her excitement." That raw difficult detail yielded the snapshot's deeper meaning: the gift of a new violin helped a daughter give some life to the mother whom time was stealing away, a mother she'd "never wished to compete with." The journal snapshot forever caught the mother's gratitude for that moment.

That Place

Our earliest memories are rooted in place: a lifetime of kitchens you've sat in, summer porches screened and curving to the night air. A grandparent's attic smelling of newspapers and wool and camphor mothballs. Old town libraries. Backyards. To remember them is to trace the route memory first took: through the senses. We first experience the world through our eyes, ears, smell, touch. In writing about place, I first always do a simple sensory prompt. It's immensely soothing, something that can shift a boring subway ride, transporting us back with the same pleasure E. B. White remembered a childhood lake in Maine — how the cabin's

72

"bedroom smelled of the lumber it was made of and of the wet woods whose scent entered through the screen."

Think of a place where, when tired, you long to return, if only in memory. (The most resonant memories often are from childhood — but not always.) On a sheet of paper, list each of the five senses. Quickly free-associate on each. What smells do you recall (roses and mildew; itchy, dry smell of stored canvas); sounds (owl in a wintry night); touch (a chenille bedspread stiff with starch); sights (V's of rust under old faucet taps); taste (first summer tomato)? In "Goodbye to All That," a black valentine to her eight years in New York before marriage, Joan Didion used such details long stored in notebooks: standing eating a peach, feeling warm subway grating air on her legs; noticing the lights above Rockefeller Center blink *Time Life* as her twenties lapsed "with the deceptive ease of a film dissolve."

Sensory details evoke the places of the past but root us in the present. No longer brooding in a journal, we now have snapshots that offer a subtler payoff: moments of illumination. "That was the year, my twenty-eighth, when I was discovering," Didion realized, "that it had all counted after all, every evasion and every procrastination, every mistake, every word, all of it . . . it is distinctly possible to stay too long at the Fair." By letting memory select the details we might have missed the first time around, these place snapshots focus the past while keeping us in the present tense.

A Single Incident

I'm sure you noticed it: how a sketch about place gets crowded. People start pacing its floors. Conversations stir. Faces glimpsed from behind banisters or seated around tables late at night come sharply into focus. Incidents — slights, successes, jealousies — are suddenly vivid. *There.* A way to narrow and not be overwhelmed by the rush of memory, is to frame a journal snapshot with a single remembered incident. It helps to think of it as a one-act play, narrowing the snapshot to a single day and place. Try to focus only on yourself and one other person. Chekhov, once asked if fiction had a future, replied, "As long as there's 'he said,' and 'she said.'" The same trick applies to journals.

Think of a specific incident in your life that, though you were probably unaware of it at the time, triggered a click in consciousness: a shift in how you viewed things differently from that moment on. Perhaps something that didn't work out quite as intended but gave you a lighter view of yourself, or a greater sense of confidence. A way to focus this snapshot is to recall when you felt yourself at a *perceived* disadvantage — being unfairly scolded by a teacher or jilted as a teenager. Evoke the incident as concretely as possible in a single page. A mini one-act scene. In journals I've seen, it's run from the comic (being called on the first time in law school) to the poignant (speaking up for a boy who was being picked on or asking an older sibling on a snowy morning if their parents were divorcing).

Invisible Snapshots

In any photo album, the most interesting pictures are often the ones missing. There are dozens of photos of my grandmother in surgical garb, for example, but hardly any of her before age seventeen. The same truth applies to memories in journals. Absences and omissions are the places where a journal's most powerful stories reside. A simple snapshot prompt I often do to uncover what memory has hidden is to write about a photo that doesn't exist *but I wish did.* Often my father is missing in family photos, since he took most of them. But snapshots develop in my journal from memory: how I wished a photo existed that caught him guiding my first steps; or of the moment, his hand invisibly suspended above mine, he let go and I stood on my own two feet.

On Della Grayson's nightstand sits a four-by-five color snapshot. It's next to a dish she puts her wrist-watch in each night so she'll see the photo at the start and end of each day. "For it should have a successor — many successors — and it has none." The photo, taken in September 1977, shows her two daughters, then nineteen and twenty-four, standing on a patio, smiling. "But of course they would be: the occasion is the reception following the wedding of the youngest, Patty, to her childhood sweetheart. The day is typical of San Diego: warm in the sun, cool in the shade. A slight breeze carries the scent of fresh-mown grass, of chicken sizzling (out of sight) on the grill near the girls. Patty's skin looks cool and flawlessly smooth; Donna's is rud-dier, as if flushed from the heat or excitement."

The real photo reminds Della of a marriage still flourishing. In the invisible photo in her journal, "what is missing, quite literally, is daughter Donna." Still alive, yet since 1991 only silence. As a mother, she can't reach her brilliant daughter who, after years of treat-ment, sometimes forgets medication. "It's her privilege to remain missing, confidentiality laws allow her this." In the meantime, the journal fills with snapshots: hope after a sighting in Los Angeles; "a friend calling anony-mously on Christmas to say she is all right for now." The family keeps active listed telephone numbers — "as long as she can remember our names, she should be able to find us." Until then, a journal thickens with snapshots waiting to show a daughter one day.

Other People

An odd thing happens in journals, which you've already noticed: the way the other people in our lives soon crowd its pages, their stories competing, even eclipsing ours. In evoking the strange richness of one's own world, many others invariably surface who need a quick sketch. Otherwise it's hard to sort your story from theirs. There's simply too much detail from others' lives. Where do you narrow the focus, how do you give your own story a clean narrative shape?

This warm-up is a version of the "objects on the tray" exercise I did as a child. Make a list of six objects most associated and the two least associated with a person. On a single journal page, empty their handbags and pockets; open drawers, cabinets, closets. Jot down what you see. It's only in your memory, so stare shamelessly, rifle through the lot. Wait. It will probably take weeks, maybe months, but snapshots will begin to emerge. Whenever you write about someone else, it's always a double portrait: of them and the you remembering them. To see how the portraits mesh takes time.

At the moment, I have my own such list — three things I took from my father's closet: octagonal onyx cuff links; a gray sweater vest; his red plaid wool bathrobe still finely matted with dog hair. Soon after my father died, I brought these home. It was a way to have him here. At the time, I knew they were somehow linked, that they said something about how he'd been quietly present. I'm still waiting for the clues to surface. The patterns are there. So, too, the stories. In the meantime, I wait, knowing that when the connections are finally made, he'll be here, past and present, joined in the transit of living memory.

EXERCISES AND JOURNAL PROMPTS

- ᴄ⃝ If you've long kept journals, go back and select ten entries you'd most regret if a journal was lost or stolen.
- ᴄ⃝ If you're just beginning a journal, which three memories would you never forgive yourself for not setting down?
- ᴄ⃝ Think of a room you've known well over three key stages in life. How did it — and you — change over time?
- ᴄ⃝ Write about your body at various intervals in your life. It, too, is a place. Do a series of snapshots: the

cardboard stiffness of new pants; the itchy feel of a school uniform; the feel of taking socks off in the middle of the night and sliding your feet between the sheets. Remember sitting at the kitchen table at ten, nineteen, thirty, sixty. Same you, different body.

CHAPTER IV

Observing the Visible World

∽

Seeing is of course very much a matter of verbalization.
Unless I call my attention to what passes before my eyes,
I simply won't see. . . . It's all a matter of keeping my
eyes open.

— ANNIE DILLARD

SATURDAY MORNINGS WE waited, a shady pause in a busy day. We sat on a wooden bench, its surface scored deeply with lovers' initials, couples who'd long since forgotten each other's name. A passerby would have seen this: a thick-set, dark-haired older woman in sensible shoes waiting for the number 11 bus. Next to her sat a girl, probably nine, coltish, uneven bangs, one sock swallowed by her shoe.

What a passerby wouldn't see as my grandmother and I waited at the bus stop was the contents of her black medical bag cratered in her lap. Only an X ray could show what I knew was inside: coupons clipped from the morning newspaper and bunched by rubber bands; powdery medicines; gauze; a lone screwdriver. Ever practical, my grandmother was ready to jimmy her way into things. You'd also need an X ray of my brain to know that, sitting there, I was slowly learning to see the world.

My grandmother Florence had an exacting eye, the price of being orphaned early in life. She knew where safety — and danger — hid. She had an instinct for seeing the incongruous. Her eye studied others clustered at the stop: a man unaware his sweater label stuck up in the back like a sales sign; the redhead's hair flat in the back from a nap, the dye job gone brassy from summer sun. Once aboard, my grandmother instinctively avoided women who held their handbags tight to their chest; vicious elbowers; anyone with sequined Christmas-wreath pins still on lapels in May. I kept my eyes on the aisles, side glancing at girls I imagined I could outrun barefoot.

Today I thought of my grandmother, as I often do, when I grabbed a notebook — this time the small one kept in my purse. I wrote. In just two city blocks, I saw a shoal of girls in plaid parochial school uniforms darting across a busy street, sleek and slippery as minnows; a man whose sweater was misbuttoned, bunching up on one side as if it had had a stroke; right after him, someone else's baby calling me Mama; across the street, a meter maid in navy shorts writing out a ticket, a purple cobra tattooed just above her heavy brown boots; nearby a dog trotting with an expensive leash, no owner. At midday, the city air smelled of a beef bouillon cube.

My grandmother's stuffed bag held everything but a notebook. Prescription pads bulged inside, but no journals. Not wanting to write about her secret childhood, she never committed to paper the things my aunt craved knowing, questions poured into her diaries: What kind of last name was that? What religion? How many years spent in that orphanage? (Questions my grandmother met with the same stare she trained on cranky patients: the silent power of refusal.) In time, I'd decode her story. Before then, I absorbed my first lessons in journals and writing. Those mornings on our way into town gave me a glorious bias in favor of the outside world. It's a great relief, writing outside the self. But soon I'd learn the secret from her: to know your own inner life, you first observe the world. Take notes. Dictation from the world, its news.

The diarist's province is the world, inner and outer. And the inner world is curiously unlocked by losing yourself first in the outside one. For most of us, it's all jumbled in one notebook, a nightmarish parody of the very chaos one is trying to escape and order. For several weeks, though, try this other way to keep a notebook: use a separate one just to observe the world. Write in crevices of otherwise lost time — waiting in bank lines, stuck in traffic. A lot gets done. This is a way to come back to the self refreshed.

The Observing World: From I to Eye

"I write entirely to find out what I'm thinking, what I'm looking at, what I see and what it means," notes Joan Didion. The way she often gets there is by stashing the seemingly random fact or observation in notebooks. Quirky items: 720 tons of soot fall on New York City annually, or a woman in a plaid silk dress sitting late morning in a railway bar, her hem coming undone. Why write it? Why bother storing? It's the hidden savings-account principle. "Some morning when the world seems drained of wonder," she says, "some day when I am only going through the motions of what I am supposed to do, which is write — on that bankrupt morning I will simply open my notebook and there it will all be, a forgotten account with accumulated interest paid passage back to the world."

A strange thing about these snapshots, all involving things observed that you store in a cheap spiral notebook: they continue working while you're not. Like rock crystals forming on a string, the details in diaries cluster. Overnight, they thicken in our minds. To rediscover them in notebooks is to quicken memory, taking us back to that exact moment our eye first noticed. *"How it felt to be me,"* says Didion, "that is getting closer to the truth about a notebook."

The significant shift that happens here is one of moving out of self-consciousness into a kind of transparency. From I to Eye. It's an essential stage, even if your primary aim in a journal is self-reflection. While eighteenth-century housewife Elizabeth Freke kept a journal *just* to record a forty-two-year miserable marriage, millions of journals are abandoned for being a joyless collection of grievances. Observing the world turns a journal from a cloudy mirror into a window. A diary kept only to record misery or complaints gives no pleasure back. For a journal to be self-renewing, it must give pleasure as well as perspective.

Do what someone I know did recently after I told her how the first step to successful journal keeping is giving a journal a specific purpose. She now keeps a separate journal marked *Spleen,* "a spectacular, satisfying array of complaints that no longer contaminate my other journals." Successful journals break the deadlock of introspective obsession. Wanting to move "away from myself into the world at large," Elizabeth Berg imagines a future journal recording "the color of sunsets, the smell of the Cozy Corner café, the substructure of flowers, bits of dialogue I overhear, outfits I see, expressions on people's faces, dogs with cuckoo ears, the flow of roof lines. That's a journal I would reread with pleasure. Because the outside world, for all its problems, is so interesting."

Shifting from self to the senses in a journal provides the same thrill as when a diarist first turns to creative projects, imagining "I" now as she or he. That journey is summed up by Gail Godwin (referring to her diary as he). "In adolescence, I weighted him down with feelings of gloom and doom; in late teens, I wasted his pages cataloguing the boys who fell into, or eluded, my snare; in my twenties, I drove him to near death-from-boredom with my lists of resolutions, budgets, and abortive plans for 'the future.' In my thirties, as my craft of fiction was consolidated . . . I returned to him with new respect. I told him when good things happened, and shared ideas for future work."

Day Visas

For a week give yourself day passes to the world. Each page represents a visa to travel and record what's in front of your eyes. It's sinfully fun, observing. It immediately disarms the Censor, who thinks you're procrastinating, and gives the procrastinator a field day of work. In reality, you're being enormously productive using all those wasted times in a day spent waiting. (At the bus stop, my grandmother made mental notes on patients, planned dinner, prayed, counted change, put stamps on bills.)

Together with the snapshots in the previous chapter, this observing notebook will give you a foundation for successful journal keeping. In less than two weeks, you'll have material to occupy you for a year. Here's how: Take a break. Sit anywhere — subway, office, coffee shop, library. Observe up to three people. (But don't stare so hard you'll get arrested.) You have ten minutes. Take reporter's notes — just lists of details. Don't write any complete sentences. Instead jot down everything specific you notice. If someone's balding, how? Hairline receding in U-shape from the crown, or a tiny back circle like a monk's tonsure? Note characteristic mannerisms — a teenager tugging a strand of hair, staring at split ends; a clerk rubbing fingers as if holding an invisible pencil.

"I don't believe I have ever gone to a doctor's office or a dentist's without a notebook," says Patricia Hampl, "the one companion I seem to require in all public and therefore potentially alien places — museums, cafés, auto body shops, wherever waiting is done." Supermarkets are good. Malls are even better. Airports, for many, are the best, "in that limbo state in between departing and arriving," says Samantha Harvey. Jot your lists. The next day open the notebook. At the top of a new page, select ten favorite observed details from yesterday. Now fill a single page imagining a scene from that person's life the moment you left. Consider the woman so carefully buying take-out supper for one. Choose one of four girls pooling their change. Think back to the teenager who kept probing his newly pierced tongue.

What you're doing is developing concrete ways to observe, and also learning how to write. Three key writing skills blossom here: notation, description, and narration. Jotting details in a list hones an instinct for the concrete. Next time out do a paragraph of description. Stare at an inanimate object — a metal filigreed ice-cream-parlor chair, for example. Describe it as if to a stranger. Now add someone to the scene.

The unsmiling girl behind the ice-cream counter, for example, afraid of showing new braces. At each stage, stay on concrete details. Without letting the Censor in, try keeping adjectives to a minimum. If you write "sad," look harder. What was it about the person? You'll see it: mouth tugging down, hands collapsed in lap.

"As I became less trapped in my universe of moods," recalls Gail Godwin, "my entries began to include more space. As a rule, I complain less and describe more; even my complaints I try to lace with memorable description." A good habit: write for an entire day without using "I."

Sharpening the Eye

After each day's visa, you'll come home (or back to your desk) with a small treasure trove. Over coffee recently, novelist Margot Livesey and I swapped odd details we've stored and later used in writing (hers often stay dormant for years in speckled composition books). Here's what to look for: strange paradoxes; sensory opposites — the kinds of things I'd poke my grand-mother's side for when noticing: how pencilled eyebrows only highlight that none exist; how slipping off just one shoe in a concert cools the entire body; how women open their mouths slightly when applying mascara.

Beginning to notice life's paradoxical details gives a deeper way to use journals. Pulitzer Prize–winning author Annie Dillard, who keeps intricately indexed journals, says, "Write about winter in the summer. Describe Norway as Ibsen did, from a desk in Italy; describe Dublin as James Joyce did from a desk in Paris. Willa Cather wrote her prairie novels in New York City."

The world often supplies its own inspirations and prompts. "I found a shopping list on the sidewalk that listed items which painted a perfect character sketch," says Cindy Riede. "I pasted it into a notebook, then made further notes about the character around it." Scavenge. Store images the world discards — orange sunglasses left in a taxi; a foreign envelope addressed to a stranger. Wait for a dry season. Open the notebook. Invent a scene.

"Inspiration," says poet David Lehman, isn't something "to sit and wait for." For him, it comes when you invite it. For two years he invited it daily. In January 1996, he started an experiment: writing a poem a day, keeping himself open to the immediacy of his busy world. Then living in New York City, "where every street seems to promise an adventure," he also traveled often as editor of *The Best American Poetry* series. Inspired by items from the newspaper or by weather, love, movies, or jazz, he wrote poems while "talking on the phone, others while waiting for dessert at a restaurant . . . a few while driving my car on the highway." Some were composed as e-mail messages, "cybernetic epistles." The "speed of composition" did more than boost productivity. It sparked "a willingness to take chances." By keeping himself open to the observed world, he practiced keeping a "poem honest by rubbing its nose in the details of daily life." The daily practice, "unpretentious as any diary entry, allows the poet to talk to the present." When culling the poems and "in shaping them into a unity of one, I had the great example of Thoreau's *Walden*." Lehman's richly reflective *The Daily Mirror: A Journal in Poetry* "provided a means to note the continuities in one's life."

The View from the Window

An observing notebook is ideal for anyone numbed by work, repetition, meetings, schedules. It's a catalyst that will reconnect us to the very living we're too busy earning to notice. Cynthia Thompson, who wrote the stolen violin snapshot, uses an observing notebook before work. A Yale Ph.D. in classics, she notes what she sees outside her window as a means of "inner rediscovery." At Stanford, Arunima Orr realized "I'd killed my own writing." The intellect was taxed. The senses starved. "I was terrified to write anything when I began, unwilling to express myself because it might not be perfect." Now a visual artist, she uses journals to sketch the immediate world, later adding words.

I liken being numbed by daily life to the brain having freezer burn. (Have you ever seen a badly frozen chicken, its edges blanched icy white? That's how I imagine a stressed brain looks.) To thaw, do what Thompson now does routinely: For five minutes take reporter's notes on the world just beyond the window. Jot as if sending a telegram *back* to the observed world. Sit for two minutes noting your senses: the itchy smell of indoor winter air; the shiver of an old fridge. What does your body feel like — the feet loose in old shoes; hands heavy in your lap. You're learning to be an antenna for feelings other than misery.

Nowhere is an "observing the world" journal better suited than as a record of a child's first two years. Like hundreds of new mothers, Zoe Nierenberg and Elizabeth Searle currently keep such journals with scientific precision. A baby's hand moving like a starfish. First words. Spontaneous stories. "I expect to share these journals with my son and daughter one day," says Nierenberg. "My own, which I only have time for every third day, are private, off-limits."

To spend twenty minutes eating lunch outside is to be fully immersed in a world. An aquarium of people. "Have I said it before? I am learning to see," Rainer Maria Rilke wrote in his classic *The Notebooks of Malte Laurids Brigge.* "It never occurred to me before how many faces there are. There are multitudes of people, but there are many more faces, because each person has several of them."

Journals astonish when we let the world astonish us. Let it in. Then, as Proust said, "The real voyage of discovery consists not in seeking new landscapes, but in having new eyes."

EXERCISES AND JOURNAL PROMPTS

☞ Take a moment to list dead spaces in a day — all the moments unexpectedly wasted today. List times when you could jump-start a journal while waiting: on the subway; before a meeting; in the car before collecting the kids; while on hold; while waiting for a meal to cook; while your baby naps.

☞ In a paragraph, describe a single scene you witnessed recently in multiple ways and from multiple perspectives. A woman, for example, being jostled by someone getting on the bus just as she's trying to get off. Do it as all verbs (jostle; collide; elbow;

swerve; curse; slap). Do it as nouns (blonde; Coke-bottle lenses; two big shopping bags). Imagine ten perspectives, ranging from amused to angry (two women wearing the same dress; one woman running into her ex-husband's new wife for the first time; one woman realizing the jostled woman interviewed her for a job the day before; one woman trying to place where she saw the other — dentist's office, day-care center, etc.).

CHAPTER V

Single-Purpose Journals

❧

*I never travel without my diary. One should always
have something sensational to read in the train.*

— OSCAR WILDE

FACTS I JOTTED as I waited yesterday: Even while sailing, Einstein scribbled notes and fragments of formulas into a pocket travel diary. Aboard the *Beagle*, Darwin filled five journals on his voyages, which shaped his theories of evolution. Da Vinci imagined the modern helicopter and submarine in notebooks he kept daily. Elias Howe invented the sewing machine in a dream he recorded the next morning. Poet and physician William Carlos Williams wrote journals and poems on prescription pads between seeing patients. Emerson kept a journal just for conversations he had with his friend William Channing, which was a wellspring of ideas for his writing.

I know what you're thinking: geniuses, the lot. It's true. Journals, though, were catalysts to their rich productivity. Even Einstein could forget. If he didn't scribble down all those x's and π's, mathematical inspiration faded. (As it did for chemist Friedrich August Kekulé von Stradonitz, whose discovery of carbon rings came in a dream he didn't record. He had to wait till he dreamt it again. *Then* he wrote it down.)

Now think back to the crowds you watched while sitting outside at lunch yesterday. Dozens of lives passed as you jotted in your observing notebook. There was that tall brunette, a tourist, ordering onion soup at the counter. A bald man spun twice in the revolving glass door. A senior citizen flagged a taxi with the tip of her walking stick. Out of the even larger passing crowd, an astonishing number keep specialized journals.

I know. I've seen hundreds and hundreds of them. The types are as diverse as the individuals who keep them: travel or genealogy journals; dream journals; family chronicles; garden notebooks; artist's sketch journals; nature or spiritual journals; joint e-mail journals; letter journals marking life's milestones.

Like Einstein and Emerson, these individuals hit

upon the secret of giving a journal a single purposeful focus. Journals don't have to be about oneself. They can be about work. Or about tracing *others'* lives — a journal kept while witnessing another's illness, for example, or while waiting for a baby to be born. From a San Francisco chef whose journals thicken with new recipes and menus to innumerable survivors who beat cancer thanks in part to projects conceived in a journal, people have found a wealth of alternatives, *expanding* ways of leaving a trace. Some I offer as seed ideas; others, as a glimpse of a life story. Innumerable lives have been changed by a journal's power to open up new worlds: books have come into being, articles published, family traces left. And in moving away from self-reflection to productivity, a writer can erase such inhibitions as perfectionism or self-censorship forever.

Travel: Journeying and Journals

Two good things happened to me in my mid-twenties. I couldn't find film in a small village in Italy; and, months later, my camera was stolen. That's how I stumbled upon the sly delight of keeping travel journals. I number these among my most prized journals. Opening a page randomly, I can summon hot afternoons in Rome, a snowy winter evening in Paris's Marais district, tiny country lanes in corners of northern Wales. A single journal transports me instantly to pale deserts, summer lakes, hidden vineyards.

"A trip," says Patricia Hampl, "has the orderliness and reassuring form of art: you depart, you experience, you return. Beginning, middle, end. In the travel journal nothing, it seems, is wasted." That built-in structure gives the journey — and life — instant narrative. It divides days into scenes, a journey into plot, allowing one to build on descriptive skills that follow so naturally from the "observing the world" journal.

Travel journals are the observing journal armed with a passport. What began as a way to occupy myself while sitting alone at tables in foreign countries quickly framed my entire experience. My journal proved more faithful than any camera. Travel not only sharpened my eye, it honed my writing skills. Almost from the start, my travel journals became a rich basis for extensive essays I published. My notes, snapshots rooted in sensory detail, provided the foundation for the finished feature article or essay.

Keep a travel journal as if writing a long letter to a close friend. By writing it for someone else's eyes, you have to supply context — place names, sights, interesting local information. (Getting home and reading "beautiful view, rural midwestern town" is as useless as a roll of overexposed photos of the view.) Travel turned artist Mary Jo McConnell into an amateur anthropologist. Documenting tribal arts from Bali to Jakarta, she began travel journals as letters to her mentor, Evelyn Bartlett, who at ninety-seven had stopped traveling herself. In time, McConnell sent on the journals — increasingly vivid reports of surviving sleeping in jungles on her travels to identify local tribal customs or handiwork.

In college, Melinda Papowitz, a politics and religion major, kept extensive journals of her time in India and Pakistan. Her weekly series of letters home, "Tales of a Reluctant Adventurer," helped conjure an endlessly exotic world for family and friends in America: drugged lizards in bazaars; mosques at midday; observing an arranged-marriage interview; the prospective bride, her skin "the color of tea brewed with a touch of milk and honey," saying with a sigh, "My heart is worrying." The saved letters, now compiled, became its own travel journal.

Travel may summon the solitary pilgrim, but often the most innovative journals are kept by couples. A retired Chicago couple recently switched from his factual log and her reflective notebook and collaborated on a travel journal in which he illustrated and she wrote around the edges of the drawings. "It gave us a common purpose. Late in marriage, people can drift apart on separate vacations or take photos but not speak." During naps or quiet times, they pooled their strengths, alternating drawing or describing. "A shared travel journal helped us discover why we'd married in the first place. We'd forgotten we *liked* taking risks, going off beaten paths. Forgot the other was so fun."

Planning a travel journal will only enrich the journey. Before setting out, fix the itinerary just inside the journal's cover. Paste a fold-out map (or Xeroxed sections of the map on several pages) and trace your route with a highlighter. While traveling, use different-colored markers charting surprise side trips. Save a good portion of the journal's blank middle pages for pasting in postcards, museum stubs, menus highlighting dishes and wines. Jot memory-triggering details (favorite works of art; location of that tiny restaurant) the same day next to each item. Keep a section listing sights or places you couldn't get to but want to return to next time.

Several couples I've met plan their travels, whether to Greece or the American Southwest, by the journals they'll amass. Returning home, instead of the inevitable slides, they have intricate, highly personalized journals to show. I've seen journals with elaborate fold-out pages; others with single themes (architecture; wildlife;

national parks; Civil War battle sites). Travel often expands a project's horizons. An idea first noted in a journal on a trip to England — swapping a house in Carmel, California, for one in Cambridge, England — led to Joan Miller's published magazine essay on her two-month experience. Mary Jo McConnell's illustrated letter and travel journals will be published as *Dear Mrs. Bartlett: Letters from the Field*. She kept her journals intact despite arduous travel by obeying three rules: never pack journals in a suitcase (they can get lost); keep journals in zippered plastic bags for climate protection; be sure a journal has acid-free paper to guarantee longevity.

The French artist Delacroix kept the most beautiful travel sketchbooks I know — pale wash-and-pen drawings of North African villages and markets, all with side commentary. Yet even an untrained hand can sketch in blank books. "During a long summer in Rome," says Samantha Harvey, "I took my sketchbook diary to the Borghese Gardens. It was a meditative way of entering that place more deeply, a way to fix images. Last summer near Venice, I came across a stone carving of two peacocks eating grain under entwined tree branches. Sitting there drawing it, with the peace of an ancient church near me, it ended up being the most memorable moment of an otherwise too hectic trip."

Nature Journals: The World at Home

All her life, my cousin Susan watched her mother, my aunt, keep diaries. Now a zoologist, Susan evolved her own kind: nature journals. Keeping them is a prized family activity, a time her husband and she share weekly with their two children, whether hiking, pulling off back roads on longer car trips, or sitting on a summer porch observing stars. They've inspired neighbors to start logs; others who at first barely know the names of anything but their own dog soon develop a keen eye for the natural world.

Nature journals not only connect us to place, they also slow us down, training us to see universes in even the tiniest corners. Almost any spot will do: forest or city park, backyard or seashore. Start with a simple focus: Trees. Tide pools. The moon in its cycles. Birds clustering at the feeder. Stars. Or, sitting quietly outside for ten minutes, describe or draw all you see: huge pillowy clouds, rustling copper beech trees, the high-pitched whirr of cicadas. Like Thoreau, try describing the same scene at several points in a day. Focus on your senses; note how subtly a landscape changes over a day.

A nature journal is a magnifying glass in words. It's the ideal way for journals to first enter kids' and parents' lives together. Choose hardcover notebooks or a clip-board with loose-leaf paper that later can be put into a binder. "It's amazing how adults lose their fear of sketching," says Susan, "by watching how easily and often well kids do it. Learn to sketch from children." The deeper value is seeing with a child's inquisitive eye: discovering why the morning's geraniums are nibbled; counting frogs slyly camouflaged in still ponds; tracing arcs of shooting stars. With their precise notations — place, time, weather, field observations — nature journals root us in our own history. A Utah father and his grown son go back to twenty years of separate nature journals, their outings always dated; so, increasingly, are notes on conversations that, for the son, happened only as his work-driven father relaxed in nature.

Garden Journals: Earthly Paradise

Years ago while renovating an old house and raising two children, an Atlanta couple's marriage was severely strained. Strangely, it was a garden journal that reseeded the marriage. They set a goal: recording three seasons in a garden (the length of time a marriage counselor suggested as a cooling-off period). He dug. She hacked back old growth. Both planned. A spiral notebook from a local stationery shop rested on a pantry shelf. Chores and successes alike had to be entered daily, in both hands. Working silently in stubborn collaboration, they cleared, planted, pruned. As the garden changed, so, slowly, did their outlooks. "Stupid as it sounds, I was standing there alone one night fighting the feeling," says the wife, "but suddenly I realized I wanted to share what I saw *with* him. Something in me had grafted back to life. I saw the garden through the eyes of a new owner. The idea of a stranger's eyes on all I'd come to feel love for again. I couldn't imagine leaving behind that garden, hard-won in so many ways."

Journals span all seasons of Alan Emett's life. For years, she kept garden logs in speckled notebooks. In Italian journals she recorded her deepening interest in New England's gardening history. Her book *So Fine a Prospect* grew from these notebooks, coalescing her own gardening skills with a deep knowledge of the area's history. Similarly, on a single day one can find landscape architect Julie Messervey redefining design in journals for her books such as *The Inward Garden*. Nearby, her daughter sits with a private diary as Julie's mother sketches them all, adding to decades of artists' sketch books that line the family shelves like photo albums.

Alexandra Johnson

Family Chronicles: Leaving a Trace for Others

Our homes are small private archives, the curator often missing: unsorted photos; old passports stamped with the names of foreign capitals; handwritten letters; thick formal documents stashed deep in drawers. It's a relief to know that genealogy software is now readily available, or that in seconds the Internet can bypass dusty archive work, tracing lives. But if ever one wished the attic had trunks of old diaries, it's when compiling more than just a factual family chronicle.

All Cathryn Griffith knew when she began sifting through memorabilia was that she was a mother at midlife, wanting to leave a chronicle for her college-age daughter, Sarah. With detective work, she discovered gold mines hidden in family trunks and languishing in relatives' drawers. She found five generations of diaries, including ones carried across the western frontier; genealogy trees; property deeds dating back centuries; stacks of yellowed newspaper clippings (her grandmother was a local politician, her mother a reporter). Scattered among them were countless photographs.

But how to organize it? Enrolling in a journal and bookmaking course at a local art college, she entered the world of desktop publishing. Within a week, she was juxtaposing photos with diary excerpts. Wasn't

104

there a more interesting way than simple chronology? Technology freed her to play with narrative, weaving stories with superimposed imagery. In doing so, she created a model for original family chronicles.

But what if you have few family records? Start them. Journals are ongoing history. A Massachusetts woman sits down weekly with her aging Greek immigrant mother. She lays out old family photos like playing cards, which instantly spark her mother's stories as she identifies the people in them. Who was he or she? the daughter asks, taking notes. How did you feel about them? What would their best friends or enemies say? Together, they diagrammed a family tree, copying it into the first page of a journal. The typed stories, often one-page biographies, filled pages.

From refugees who've fled war-torn Europe or Asia, I've seen journals re-created by using the "missing photograph" prompt discussed in chapter 3. Armed with tape recorders, descendants ask parents or grandparents to reflect on lost worlds. (The "object description exercise" in chapter 3 is also an excellent memory trigger.) Each gathered family member is asked to begin his or her reflections with: *What I remember.* Immediately after, others can answer the question, *What is still missing from that story?*

Other ways to leave a trace. A family spread over

three continents keeps a monthly round-robin of e-mail letters placed in separate journals. A divorced Wyoming father sends his twelve-year-old daughter living in another state letter journals. "It's different from e-mail. I want her to have a permanent record of trust, something that won't vanish with a delete key." A British-born mother tape-recorded her son's Cockney accent before it became Americanized; in a separate notebook, she jotted down Cockney slang and lore he'd need to appreciate her heritage.

Similarly, with a notebook in his lap, a newly retired insurance broker turned stacks of home videos into a summer project. Home videos are the diaries we're too busy to keep. But without commentary, they're like faded photos without identification on the back. As his first retirement project he kept journals *retrospectively*, identifying relatives or family friends for his grandchildren, filling in the context of a world before they were born.

Studs Terkel is the master of oral histories. Three years ago, he wasn't surprised when I told him how others had found ways to keep journals for those who couldn't. I told him of the Detroit son who began an Alzheimer's journal for his father, getting down memories while he still remembered. (Four million Americans currently are affected by the disease.) Similarly, what began as a visit to a great-grandmother in a nursing home soon became a collective summer project for Lucy Goodman, who enlisted her college friends as part of a community commitment. "I saw all those old people in wheelchairs parked next to each other in windowless corridors. TVs blaring. No one asking them about their lives." Spending twenty minutes a week, Goodman recorded stories in spiral notebooks, saving them for relatives or donating them to the home's growing story library. For the college students, it linked individual lives to world history, immersing them in firsthand accounts of both world wars, immigration, the Depression. "It gave history a face," says Lucy, "and gave so many lives back theirs."

History is passed on in other ways. Among my favorite such journals is one composed exclusively of family recipes from Italy's Abruzzi region. Pasted at the top of a journal page is a photo of each cook — grandmother, mother, great-aunt, cousins. Short biographies in Italian and English follow. The centerpiece is recipes. Eleven copies of the original journal were sent to extended family. The recipes now grace tables from New York to Los Angeles, giving the family terrific food as well as conversation about how they're part of a living chain of cooks.

Dreaming the Work

For two decades, Patrick Morton, a professor of mathematics at Wellesley College, has kept dream journals in hardbound blank books. "I first became consciously involved with my dreams in graduate school. A few of the dreams had a rudimentary mathematical content. Mathematical symbols had been filling up my imagination for a long time already, so the beginning dreams used anything they could to represent what they wanted me to be aware of."

In 1979, while working on his doctoral dissertation, "I realized my unconscious was helping me solve the problems I was engaged in." A dream woke him at 2 A.M. "In it, a whirling energy mass turned into a human head and said to my adviser and me: 'You've found the answer!'" For three days he felt "heightened anticipation." Aware of "a very powerful energy building inside of me, I could literally feel it undergoing some process of gestation. I kept working on the problem without exactly understanding what the hint meant to 'use Abelian fields.' I managed to discover the key step three days later, which led to my whole thesis." Since then, he alternates between logs and interpretive commentary. "Notice that even in this dream the answer came only as a very powerful hint. I had to figure out the details myself."

As a child, Sandy Khan solved math problems by asking for the solutions just before she went to sleep. In time, she gave up a successful teaching career to start a business conceived, of course, in a dream. Now a book binder, she transforms old books, a business that's spawned a specialty journal shop based in Cambridge, Massachusetts. Its walls are lined with journals fitted inside covers of beautiful old books: daily logs, blank books, dream journals, spiritual journals, nature journals.

To begin keeping a dream journal, she suggests planting questions subconsciously just before sleep. Always have a pen and journal near the bed. Record and date even fragments of dreams immediately. Adds Patrick Morton, "Don't wake up with a loud alarm." Dream symbols, he stresses, deepen in time. "Instead of asking for a meaning, ask for a new image to come in a dream that expands on the original image. There is a definite progression in dreams, specific signposts, markers of progress."

Crisis Journals: Doing the Unexpected with the Unexpected

Each life has its own crisis times: a marriage or job ends; a parent is widowed; a child falls into trouble. Journals are invaluable allies when life takes unexpected turns. Numerous such stories about life patterns are threaded into the chapters in part 2, showing ways others transformed factual logs into richer reflections on what life brings. For Maria Judge, a dean at the Fletcher School of Law and Diplomacy at Tufts University, it was illness. Immediately after being diagnosed with breast cancer, she began a one-year journal, the length of her treatment and recovery.

For Maria, as for other cancer survivors, a journal gives a sense of control, the very thing illness takes away. It records decision making, and provides a necessary distance as well as a safety valve for emotions. Inspired by May Sarton's published journals chronicling illness over a single year, Maria Judge kept hers on a computer, printing pages into a loose-leaf binder, marking fifty-day intervals.

But even during early medical consultations, she says, "I realized that a scene I was describing in the journal would make a good picture." From the start, she decided on a series of photographs kept in tandem with the journal. Two journal projects: one private, one public. "I arrived at my first chemo treatment with my camera. Not only did the doctors, nurses, and technicians see me in a different light, but I also experienced treatment differently." She stresses how having a purpose and taking control via a journal can help millions of cases like hers. "The fact that I chose to take pictures of these daily routines shifted the focus (for me and others) away from the disease itself and onto the human story behind it, which often gets lost amid the fear, confusion, discomfort, and, ultimately, the routine of treatment. It allowed other things to come through: humor, irony, insight, demystification, manageability."

Noting situational incongruities (smoking areas in hospitals; strange names of some staff members), she slowly filled her tandem journal with photos. "I didn't reflect so much on the photographs as the scenes behind them." Humor, as much as strong family support, helped heal her. Among the photos: Maria, pretreatment, posing with bald male colleagues, "thinking ahead a few weeks to when I expect to look like them." A giggling three-year-old nephew, delighted "he had four aunts" in Maria, all with different hair or hats. A groomed wig tossed on a doorknob or a vacuum cleaner as spontaneity increasingly mattered more than appearance. A year after Maria's full recovery, the photos (with moving, often witty, journal captions) went on traveling exhibit.

Often challenges around illness are a catalyst to significant projects or published work that comes out of journals. Mimi Schwartz, a college professor, first published a now widely anthologized essay in *Lear's* magazine on surviving breast cancer. "Journal writing — and the process of turning it into a public account — made all the difference for me in recovering quickly, emotionally and physically. It gave me a double set of survival goals: health and telling the story." Using her journal's notes, she shifted from academic to narrative writing, a shift that sparked a new career project — contributing essays regularly to the creative nonfiction journal *Fourth Genre*.

It's not just a patient who benefits by journal keeping, but also the family or friends witnessing a loved one's illness. A journal siphons private fears and dramas into the page, allowing others to focus their emotional energies on the patient. Long term, it provides an invaluable reminder of human resilience. Ten years after her husband, architect Bruce Greenwald, successfully beat cancer, Karen Horowitz combed extensive diaries she'd kept then as well as at twenty-one, when her mother battled the disease. She drew heavily on them for her book *Witnessing Illness*, which offers practical coping strategies. At forty-one, Robert McCrumb, editor in chief of London's Faber and Faber publishing house, suffered a stroke. His book *My Year Off* excerpts the parallel diaries he and his wife kept as they moved from tragedy to recovery. In *Thanksgiving,* Elizabeth Cox used a journal as a life-line chronicle, a surviving parent's record for a son too young to remember losing a father to AIDS.

Marking Life's Milestones

On the cusp of turning fifty, Katya Taylor designed a single-purpose journal: a friendship album journal. Along with family, "friendships had been the key element" in her life. Four months before her January birthday, she wrote to thirty-five friends, asking each to write a short letter. She, in turn, wrote a letter to them. Letters poured in from friends all over the country, many not seen in years. All but one contributed on time. Placing each letter received side by side with the one she composed, she added photos and sent each friend a copy of the journal.

Her journal's success soon inspired her parents to plan a journal celebrating their fiftieth wedding anniversary. Katya helped, contacting one hundred of their friends, asking them to contribute a single memory or story connected to that friendship. Some tips: "I gave them the starting phrase, 'I first met'; I made sure they knew to leave margins so the letters could be inserted into the album pages; I put a firm 'please return by this date,' making it even earlier than needed."

Two years after Carolyn Livingston's husband died, she marked milestones in a journal by writing a letter to him on significant dates: birthdays, anniversaries, the anniversary of his death. In another journal, wanting to leave her three grown children a *living* record, she compiled "Flashbacks and Random Thoughts," a collection of snapshots, sketches, and reflections on milestones she'd crossed as a senior citizen. In its preface she wrote, "I think of my parents and grandparents and wonder what they were really like, what they thought and how they felt. Were they always the personas they displayed to me? Did they sometimes feel intimidated by their children's feelings and reactions towards them? Did they ever want to express feelings they could not, or would not? I imagine so — most of us do."

A Gratitude Journal and Many Others

Single-year journals charting life's transitions — marriage, new baby, career switch, divorce, retirement — often spark companion journals. Reading journals list books or practical advice that helped. Commonplace books compile favorite quotations. Wildly popular in the nineteenth century (Emerson consulted his almost daily), commonplace books are kept now by millions of people to inspire or console during dry or difficult seasons in a life. Often it's the only journal busy people can keep — a quick way to renew the spirit and keep it focused. Hillary Rodham Clinton, for example, has long kept commonplace books, filling them with favorite quotes "to derive support from what somebody else has gone through and how they articulated it." Spiritual journals often grow directly out of commonplace books. All faiths have such journal traditions. Lida Maxwell, now in law school, simply begins her entries by copying out a single quotation or verse to get herself going. "It's a way of keeping perspective, mapping life's inner quest amid the notations of a busy external life."

If I could keep only two journals, it would be the "observing the world" journal and a journal of gratitude. In the tradition of Quaker diaries, Oprah Winfrey has long kept a daily gratitude journal. "I have kept a journal since I was fifteen years old. As I've grown older, I have learned to appreciate living in the moment." At night, she lists a minimum of five things she's grateful for — no matter how small. She says it's been instrumental in her success. "What it will begin to do is change your perspective of your day and your life. I believe that if you can learn to focus on what you have, you will always see that the universe is abundant."

Keeping a journal is one of the few ways to remind oneself of life's unnoticed gifts. There are millions of ways to give journals — and life itself — a purpose. Full of surprises, journals help us bear witness as well as astonish. In doing so, they are like found money.

EXERCISES AND JOURNAL PROMPTS

⌒ Collecting oral histories or life stories from people in nursing homes makes an ideal community journal project. Start the interview by writing down the subject's birthdate and place of birth, names of parents and siblings, education, and work experience. To elicit stories, ask such questions as, What are your earliest memories? Who had the greatest influence on you (parents, teachers, mentors)? When did you realize you had an important skill or talent? What challenge were you most proud of overcoming? What do you feel are the most important lessons to be passed on to the next generation? What so far has been your greatest joy?

⌒ Ask the same questions of the older generation in your own family.

☞ Make a companion journal by filling in the context for home videos. With another family member, note separately details or stories that are important. Compare lists. Take turns writing the final journal entry, each doing every other video. If the videos are destroyed, you'll still have a life record.

PART TWO

TRANSFORMING A LIFE
Patterns and Meaning

~

*A person's work is nothing but a long
journey to recover, through the detours
of art, the two or three simple and great
images which first gained access to their
hearts.*

—ALBERT CAMUS

CHAPTER VI

Seeing Again: Finding Hidden Patterns in a Life

⤝

Gaining access to that interior life is a kind of . . .
archaeology: on the basis of some information and a little
bit of guesswork you journey to a site to see what remains
were left behind and you reconstruct the world.

— TONI MORRISON

FRESH FROM A good night's sleep, my grandmother read the obituaries, clipping them like coupons with a pair of pinking shears she kept tucked in the pocket of her cotton housecoat. On times I'd stay over, we'd sit in the morning, separate newspaper sections falling in accordion pleats across our laps. The obituaries were the first section my grandmother always turned to. "Cheap biography," she'd proclaim. She scanned less for someone she knew than for lives that fed that probing mind of hers. Watching the quick, liquid movement of those eyes, I knew we were after the same thing: hidden clues.

Those weekend mornings, I'd read the children's section, studying my favorite puzzle of two seemingly identical drawings. In the one on the right, though, items were missing — a feather in a cap, a chimney, an eyebrow, a blackbird singing in a tree. My eye moved back and forth, carefully searching for what had been omitted. By the time I'd finished, so had my grandmother. Before her was a neat stack of obituaries, their edges zigzagged. Invariably, she'd cracked the code of omissions like "cause of death unknown." ("Diabetes," she'd stage-whisper.)

Long before I began keeping journals my grandmother was training me not to get lost in facts, but to find the more interesting story hidden behind them. Simply by sitting next to her, I was learning my very first lessons in detecting life patterns. Look for the omissions, she'd say, holding a stack of clippings, look for the incongruous details: litigating stepchildren, untraceable lost years, the lightning pause between marriages. These were the real stories behind the obituaries' "facts."

It would take years for me to discover hers. And by then it would be by crafting the eulogy I'd give at her memorial. (I like to think how pleased she'd be that I spotted the telling omissions in her own obituary. It was far too neat. This was not helped by my own mother shaving three years off my grandmother's real age of ninety-four. But which three years had been lost? The first secret orphanage years she spent between ages two and five? The two summers she was boarded with foster families before being returned to the orphanage at nine? The bouts of childhood malaria she relived while dying?) It's not surprising that in time I'd keep diaries, become a writer, teach memoir. What else for someone trained in reading obituaries and finding missing puzzle clues? Those childhood weekends gave me a keen interest in narrative, in life stories. But also in figuring out deep patterns of meaning in journals.

A journal is always a self-portrait, its narrative still evolving. The story of any living diarist's life is in flux, its ending yet to be written. "Do you think that's how he imagined his life?" my grandmother often asked (usually after reading an obituary of someone who'd run off from his first family and bankrupted his second). Her advice: make sure the final version of a life story is the one you'd want to tell yourself.

A journal gives you that chance. It gives you the time to tell and *reframe* a life's story. Years ago I met a man who began his first diary at sixty-seven, before successful heart surgery. "I'd never thought about keeping a journal until I realized I might die. So I kept it just before and after the bypass. Six months later, I realized the portrait I was leaving for my family wasn't the whole picture. They'd never know what I'd learned, not just from the illness but way before it. What mattered to me."

Finding the Patterns

No matter how raw or incomplete, journals are already full of patterns. Even the "observing the world" journal offers a diarist invaluable clues to those patterns simply by being a record of what the eye selected or kept coming back to. A Florida woman noticed that her observing journal's most frequent (and longest) descriptions were of children. It clarified her desire not to delay starting a family. A New Yorker noticed that his nature journals recorded him at his happiest, evidence that he should reconsider an urban life.

This section offers ways to begin transforming a diary from a factual log into deeper reflection. Anyone who's kept a journal for even two months has enough material to find countless patterns. Anytime you've set down ten facts or described a single memory, you've

124

begun to tell a story. It takes a second glance — sometimes just after you've written, but often years later — to see the story clearly.

Dag Hammarskjöld, the second secretary-general of the United Nations, kept factual logs for years. A trained mountain climber, he titled his memoir *Markings*, referring to the tracks left by his footprints. The markings were also key life patterns he'd noticed when combing his journals to write his memoir. Identifying important life points is crucial to beginning to unlock the stories deep within journals. The first way to identify such markers is to notice how often material falls into set categories. (Only after keeping my own journals for years did I recognize that my grandmother had routinely decoded lives by fitting information into specific categories. Her favorites were illness, marriage, and death.)

Journals contain ten categories of life patterns: longing; fear, mastery; (intentional) silences; key influences; hidden lessons; secret gifts; challenges; unfinished business; untapped potential. Each category corresponds to a way we engage or hold back in life. To begin to see a journal through these ten organizing devices is to unknot years of tangled entries. It's most helpful if you go back through journals first by posing each life pattern as a *question*. Where, for example, are incidents of mastery? They may be in work, school, raising children. Or how was conflict a secret gift, highlighting potential that was still untapped?

For a diarist from St. Paul, Minnesota, two patterns stood out as she reread journals she'd kept only sporadically. Saddled with an impossible mother-in-law, she suddenly saw years of mastery hidden behind the misery. Being tested by a perfectionist mother-in-law, in retrospect, turned out be a strange gift: she learned to speak up. That led to greater independence in general. With a new eye, she began a journal in the form of letters to remind herself in the future of what to do when *she* had a daughter-in-law.

In looking to identify and separate patterns, it's useful to take a different-colored pencil to highlight categories. Underline or bracket corresponding passages. You can also keep a separate journal with sections devoted to the individual categories, such as mastery or secret gifts. When a Silicon Valley systems analyst looked over a factual log journal he'd kept right after college, for example, he realized that leaving a job had been a secret gift. He'd hated the job, but had been afraid to give up his financial security. He traced all the subsequent steps toward mastery encoded in the log: returning to graduate school; hatching a new software idea; courting venture capitalists who helped him start his own company with two fellow students. While he still now keeps a daily factual log, he also has a separate journal just for three categories: challenges, untapped potential, and mastery.

Journals and Decision Making

Journals are databases of decision making. Each of the ten categories just mentioned corresponds to a way we act directly or hold back in life. One of the quickest ways to unlock specific patterns is to look for moments when *not* making a particular decision changed your life. When a Florida mother, for example, decided not to return to work after the birth of her daughter, she feared losing a foothold in her career. Returning to that original decision in a now ten-year-old journal, she discovered through subsequent entries how her fear became a catalyst for mastery, specifically, successfully balancing motherhood and a career.

The best way to produce a rich pattern inventory is to trace how one gained a sense of mastery or self-confidence. Clues are often hidden in entries recording conflict or difficulty. Mary Brandt, a pediatric surgeon, has years of diaries, inspired by a father who kept them all his life. Recently, she explored a single incident and saw it blossom into two stories with a deeper pattern.

When she was a less-than-confident surgical resident in an E.R., Mary had to operate on an eight-year-old girl who'd been hit by a truck. It was the first time Mary had opened a chest.

For ten minutes one afternoon she sketched a single journal snapshot of that event. A deeper memory emerged: "How I grabbed her heart between my hands, shouting orders to everyone around me. I climbed onto the stretcher, straddling her body, my hands rhythmically squeezing her heart. I periodically stopped my massage as her heart would start on its own. And then stop." In the diary she'd noted how she coached the girl, "Come on, come on." Seeing that phrase triggered a parallel memory that had been buried for years. Miscalculating a lake's distance while she was swimming as a child, Mary panicked, fearing she wouldn't make it to shore. But every ten strokes, as rhythmically as she'd later coach her future patient, she remembered "hearing my father's voice say, *'You can do it.'* Somewhere deep inside I suddenly, unequivocally, knew I would." That pattern of persistence, "the place where strength resides, where fear gives way," led her to find entries of why — and how — she'd become a surgeon. It also explained why encouraging others was so easy for her in life.

Cherie Taylor has always been willing to go against set opinion. She noticed a pattern of mastery when she looked at times of decision making: deciding to go to law school, deciding to give up private practice, deciding to join the law faculty of a major Texas university. In her current journal she added something she'd never before recorded. The new entry was sparked by seeing patterns emerge from old journals. It was a single memory: "Sitting in the last row. Late afternoon. 4th grade, Satchelford Elementary. Miss Peters asking our adult ambitions. Before me went a long string of others. The boys: doctor, fireman, football player, policeman, car dealer. The girls: nurse, mommy, teacher, mommy. I knew when I stood up it would surprise. After all, it was not as if the fourth grade required much of me, the real me, to come out. I took a breath and blurted it out before I was fully on my feet, dangerous, because I was clumsy. Total silence. Then a boy yelled out, 'You can't do that.' 'Why not?' I yelled back. 'Girls are not lawyers,' he said as I sat down. 'Girls can be anything,' I said." That memory of first standing her ground also gave her clues to how she'd later *kept* her self-confidence: humor, learning to trust that adversity galvanizes her.

Clicks in Consciousness

Buried even in sporadic or all-complaining journals are key moments, so called as they unlock deeper life patterns stored in a journal. These are moments that signal a click in consciousness. If journals are often begun to record seismic shifts in a life, they also contain subtler patterns indicating when a shift is *about* to happen. How to find them? In Chinese, the ideogram for "crisis" means both danger and opportunity. In journals, look for entries where *both* danger and opportunity appear. These are what I call "tension points": moments, however brief, when two consciousnesses — one old, one new — first compete. When we realize ways of being are under new consideration.

Rather than combing old journals, there's a simpler way to access key moments. Once again, write a narrative snapshot, two pages maximum. Recall a single incident when you were at a real or *perceived* disadvantage in life. It may be comic (a teenage date gone awry), or heartbreaking (giving a baby up for adoption). The trick is to keep the focus narrow: just two people (you and that miserable fourth-grade math teacher), one setting (dusty classroom); one day. What was the sudden insight or revelation? Not making Phi Beta Kappa in college triggered for Joan Didion a series of deeper insights on self-respect. "I lost the conviction that lights would always turn green for me, the pleasant certainty that those passive virtues which had won me approval as a child automatically guaranteed me . . . happiness, honor."

Just by noting the day's events, a journal contains dozens of single-incident scenes, summarized rather than fully depicted. The patterns are there, but the entries are like slides out of order. This was the case for long-time diarist Audrey Lee, a Philadelphia statistical typist who briefly fell between life's cracks. Due to health and part-time work issues, "I was homeless from November 1981 to September 1982." In her journal she noted, "I had a ring full of keys to doors I no longer had access to; locks I'd installed and had to leave behind."

In the most harrowing circumstances, a journal helped her keep her dignity and offered a clear picture of who she really was. "After six months of living in other people's places, I realized how important a journal was. I had fears of losing my identity. There, in a ragged room, doors askew, the diary was always with me, keeping a record." Worried about losing the journal, she took it when "I'd go down to the river, trying to think a way out of my homelessness. I'd write about the day's events. Only later, when I reread those journal notes, I saw reflected back the hardiness I had as an individual that saved me."

The journal contained a series of patterns: challenge,

fear, mastery. Eating at McDonald's, she noticed she was trying to create a sense of home with "napkins spread over my table for a cloth." Yet she also recorded "an obviously homeless woman" at a nearby table making an inventory of possessions. "I recognized myself becoming her." One journal entry set a pattern she later labeled: *crossroads*. For her, they were literal and symbolic. "Waiting for a bus one bitterly cold day at the intersection of a highway to take me to temporary work," she noticed that "behind where I stood was a stonemason's shop. I saw one grave marker with the name Audrey on it. Just the name, no dates of birth or death. It bothered me, since I have an imagination." Seeing her own name began entries with a new theme: using untapped potential.

As always, she began a new journal "at midnight into the new year." The first entry: "I began the new year homeless. My need is to relaunch myself." To do so, she searched for earlier examples of hardiness in her journal. She underlined lessons she'd learned: "Avoid acting from desperation; it leaves one open to compromises that one might otherwise not make — staying anywhere shelter is offered, no matter how unhealthy the house and its occupants."

Recalling how she discovered Thoreau in night college, she began keeping a quotation journal, *Fragments*, to keep her attitude positive. An avid reader, while seeking books in the local public library on job skills, she discovered poet W. H. Auden's "My Belief." One quote became a motto: "People are happy and good who have found their vocation: what vocations there are will depend upon the society within which they are practiced."

Long after finding work in a legal firm, she uses a journal now to note new patterns: "appreciating my chair, because it once was the only one"; "noticing sunlight on a bedspread, knowing there is no life without shadows." While the uncertainties of aging crop up in the journal now, she often returns to a poem she wrote when homeless. Its last line is "Grace goes on eternally caring for her own image."

Key life patterns emerged strangely for a reluctant first-time journal keeper. These were almost not recorded during a stay in a church-run shelter, where she'd taken her three-year-old son, fleeing physical abuse. "Everything was logged. One of the administrators gave my son a spare notebook to color in. I ignored one they gave me. But later, to fill time, I began a kind of log. All I had was a ballpoint pen with runny blue ink. When it dried up, I borrowed someone else's pen. A week later I got back to the journal. I wanted to record things my son was saying, like not being so afraid. Feeling safe. When I opened it, all I saw was the ink, not the words. Just the ink: black and blue. Black and blue. I can't tell you why, but seeing that took my breath away like nothing else so far. I got it. Pages that looked like bruises that could have been my future. Seeing it, I saw I *had* to do something about it." The weekly journal became a way to shore up confidence, record newly mastered steps. Now kept as a future record for her son, noting patterns of "health and gratitude," the log is written in green ink. "To remind me I'm able to support us all on my own."

Facts and Deeper Truths

While these stories are dramatic, every journal has its own tales to tell. Often, though, the extraordinary is hidden in the ordinary fact. Stories are buried or omitted. "One can't record everything in a day," says memoirist and Harvard professor Susan Suleiman. "The mind or imagination is constantly making choices, its own selections." Rereading, you see how much you've preselected — and therefore left out. A quick way to access buried or omitted details in journals is to highlight key facts — a date you canceled, an old friend you ran into — and reconstruct the fuller days or memories the facts stand for. Do it as a snapshot. Supplying description will trigger surprisingly rich recollections. If you keep a daily factual log, do a weekly summary of what was most important. From that, list key patterns you notice. Each month, compare the lists.

"When I find I'm not writing in my journal daily," says Cindy Riede, "I know I'm shut down in some way and that I need to wake up and pay attention." One way to find key life markers is to reread your journals at the end of the year. January is named after Janus, the Roman god of beginnings and endings. End the old year and begin the new by listing life shifts and setting pattern goals. A Philadelphia woman training to be a rabbi keeps journals for two important holidays: Rosh Hashana, or Jewish New Year, and Yom Kippur, or Day of Atonement, reflecting on gifts and lessons.

Patterns Hidden Within Patterns

Often life circumstances dictate recording only one ongoing event. The birth of a baby. A new job or career. A marriage that ends. Yet for Suzanne Weeks, a writer for public television, recurrent illness never obscures the patterns of mastery and creativity she credits with her survival. Having dozens of detailed journals to refer to — full of patterns of past decision making and survival skills — helped her "motivate and heal" during recent surgery for a brain tumor. Her multiple use of journals in such a crisis is a technique millions can benefit from: using a current journal as a way to distance oneself "from the immediacy of illness"; referring to past journals to help "make practical decisions in health care, sorting options logically, less emotionally." Decisions are made by referring to patterns in past journals. "It is *very* helpful to read past journals and know that I *survived*."

A journal keeper for three decades, Weeks read Anne Frank's diary as a child, struck by "the grace that could be achieved by choosing to bring observation to the grimmest of circumstances." Since "illness disrupts life chronologically," she keeps a pocket notebook at home or on a hospital nightstand. "I write key words and phrases to spark my memory later on. I've also drawn time lines and medical tables to extract thoughts later. Any paper will do — surgical fact sheets, for example. The muse appears often during illness, but he / she doesn't often speak in full sentences."

Rereading journals that recorded surgery information was "helpful weeks later, since memories were no longer fuzzy due to drugs. Writing on the effects of treatment is necessary in retrospect." So was being reminded of long-term decision making. She realized the wisdom of opting for intensive chemo when she'd secured job tenure, how it allowed her to use the second half of a paid leave to complete a book interrupted by illness. For that, "I wanted to look for patterns of denial or acceptance of my situation." Questions she poses to elicit patterns: What do I most want out of my life? What is this illness taking most from me? What is it giving me?

Keeping commonplace journals guides her in both illness and health. A sampling of her quotations: "Every grief or inexplicable seizure — if we discipline ourselves and think hard enough — can be turned into account" (May Sarton). "Talent in the highest and broadest sense means talent for life" (Boris Pasternak). The one that recurs most frequently is: "The best way out is always through" (Robert Frost). Choosing a past journal, she compares how the various quotes apply to her current situation. "The ones that offer inspiration continue, yet how others differ now is a way to explore in a new journal entry."

She often begins a daily entry by freewriting on one of these quotations for fifteen minutes. "Illness sometimes produces a feeling of becoming a non-self. Writing, holding the pen, draws a surge of energy from the air that reinforces the truth — not merely the fact — that I am alive. Writing down my observations, recounting a doctor visit, sorting through confusion, is a means of continuing to define and affirm myself daily." In a recent journal entry she noted: "I have a job and house I've always dreamed of; energy, hair, and even a weight that is finally normal. I have bad days, bitter and angry, but I realize happiness now is a choice."

Back home again, it's a relief for her to return to the observing world journal. A recent entry: "A tumult of moments: the trees budding in Harvard Yard. The voices of children. The joyous 4-footed tread of cats and dogs. Love. The giant round capsule I am laid in while whirring lenses take images. This, Easter weekend, 6 yrs to the day since my first cancer surgery, another full circle."

Journals, like the life they record, are present tense. When we finally see their patterns, we reimagine our lives. Each page is a stepping-stone, helping us cross to safety.

EXERCISES AND JOURNAL PROMPTS

☞ Select a single journal entry or think back to a specific incident that, although you probably weren't aware of it at the time, shaped how you *now* view your life. It doesn't have to be an earth-shattering lesson or revelation. It might be a situation in which you gained a sudden sense of confidence. Or one in which you took a much lighter view of yourself after something didn't work as planned. Write a one-page sketch of the incident. Reread it two days later. Note the shift in life patterns you see from that moment till now. What was the hidden lesson? The secret gift?

☞ Do the single-incident snapshot for several key stages of your life. An ideal focus is a time when you were at a perceived disadvantage, or when an incident triggered new insights that changed the way you view the world. Let these successive incident snapshots frame a new journal.

☞ If you write on only one side of a journal's pages, pick an entry and in a different ink use the flip side to explore what was omitted in the entry. What wasn't said. What that day's events set into motion.

CHAPTER VII

Beginning to Connect the Patterns

∽

Writing is one way of discovering sequence in experi-
ence. . . . Connections slowly emerge. Like distant land-
marks you are approaching, cause and effect begin to
align themselves. . . . Experiences . . . connect and are
identified as a larger shape.

— EUDORA WELTY

"WINTER, ENDLESSLY. Still snowing. Indoors, the bed's a blizzard of Kleenex. Small crumpled mounds, dirty white like the snow clinging stubbornly to every surface of New England."

Four sentences, as anemic as I felt late one afternoon. Home with a miserable mid-January cold, it's all I could manage writing in a journal. I was in that twilight state: ill enough not to be at work or at my desk, but well enough to want to do something with my mind. (Guiltily, I recalled how in his college diary, novelist John Gardner practiced five styles of writing *about* having a bad cold.) But writing that day was clearly out. So was serious reading. Television only made me sleepier; I'd save it for evening. It was then I remembered the carton filled with my old journals stashed in the closet. I'd never unpacked it, although I'd owned the house for months. On that snowy New England afternoon I pulled them out, the stack uneven, ill-sorted. On the top was a five-year-old commonplace quotation book. Wasn't this the time to use it? Dry seasons in a life — illness, boredom, blankness?

As if in eerie reply, the first quote I read was one I'd copied from May Sarton's *Journal of a Solitude:* "I always forget how important the empty days are, how important it may be sometimes not to expect to produce anything, even a few lines in a journal. I am still pursued by a neurosis about work inherited from my father. A day where one has not pushed oneself to the limit seems a damaged, damaging day. Not so. The most valuable thing we can do for the psyche, occasionally, is to let it rest, wander, live in the changing light of a room."

I'd forgotten how true that advice was. I began idly flipping through the other volumes. To reread a journal,

I suspected, was to set yourself up for double misery: finding no wisdom and seeing how awful the original writing was. Yet I felt a quiet shiver of surprise. They weren't so bad. Scenes blossomed in memory from a single fact like those Japanese paper flowers I'd toss in the bottom of a bowl as a child. I felt a strange fondness for this someone else in the journal. (I *was* someone else then.) Life, as Annie Dillard says of her own journals, *had* accumulated, not merely passed. My cold seemed to disappear. Suddenly grateful for the hours of quiet stretching before me, I began to read for patterns, simple ways to index. An hour in, I began to see where the stories were.

But like slides tossed in a box, they were all out of order. "The accumulation of entries produces, gradually, the sense of several stories unfolding for the writer," says Susan Suleiman. "As I begin to realize that my diary is producing a series of stories, I allow those stories to determine the further direction of my diary. I am moving closer to what a novelist does."

The next stage of diary keeping is to focus and reframe patterns, to begin to line up stories. Patterns and persistent memories are scattered not just in diaries but in writers' notebooks and observing world, travel, and dream journals. "When I write in my diary," says Perri Klass, "that telling is itself a gesture toward consciousness and control. If you keep a diary, you live a narrated life, and a narrated life is intrinsically different; it has an extra layer."

Indexing

How to lift that extra layer, skimming it like fresh cream? Most journals, says Patricia Hampl, are "passionately written but virginally unread." (Except hers, which proved helpful when writing her first two memoirs.) The first way to focus patterns and group material is simple indexing. For me, that's a word that summoned the panic of making sixth-grade outlines, worrying about where the Roman numerals should go. That's until I met Ray Zager, a retired lawyer, whose first diary was "a bar mitzvah gift in 1937. It was a five-year pocket diary with less than an inch to write in. My first entry was the score of the UCLA and USC football game." He now has a library of more than sixty-five journals, indexed and cataloged by year. "My journals are all indexed so all that went in can be found and used."

Inspired by Emerson, who started a diary at sixteen at Harvard, Zager adopted his system. "Emerson knew the value of recorded information. His father and grandfather were both diarists. In order not to lose time looking for an item, he indexed them." Though seventy-four, Zager still has a good memory. "It's wonderful to have an index. Put my diary on the witness stand, test its memory. What does one index? People's names, names of places, dreams, illnesses, dialogues, feelings, friends, relatives, questions, my teachers, the law, funerals, childhood stories." To scan an index is to find: "a trip to Haifa, the happiness of finding a lost diary, solitude, Ma's Passover table, my dearest friend's death, pleasures of the mind, slowing down a law practice."

His indexing method is an excellent one. Reserve the last three pages of a diary. With a ruler, draw two lines, dividing each page vertically and horizontally. This will yield four rectangles per page. Within each box, group two to three letters of the alphabet. Certain letters will have more entries than others. (A, B, C, S, and T usually need a box of their own as so many words begin with them.) For example, when Ray writes "D" and "E" in a single box, every item beginning with either letter gets entered. He indexes current journals every fifteen pages, making it part of his recording routine.

In his retirement, Ray's indexed journals have proven invaluable. "I wanted to write an article about Egypt. My memory knew the places: Karnak, the Nile, Luxor, Cairo. I know the year, so check the volume.

Eureka! The volume is filled with Egypt, and each major item is in the index." Most recently, they were essential for him when he wrote a memoir of his World War II experiences as a motor messenger with the U.S. Seventy-first Infantry Division.

Cindy Riede, completing an M.F.A degree in creative writing, uses similar indexing. "I find it interesting to look back in journals to see how stories or poems developed." To trace a novel's first stages, for example, she finds it by title in the index, then sticks Post-it notes on relevant journal pages for quick scanning. Wanting to rework a short story written years ago, she found the "early seed for the story. I found the lists I'd made for it, questions I'd jotted down, idea clusters. Seeing it gave me great respect and gratitude for the process of keeping a journal." As Gail Godwin puts it, "I know one of us has it — my diary or me — and so, if I can't remember something, I look it up."

Uncovering Key Details

Here are two simple but effective ways to begin focusing loose material and patterns: look for entries that return to a persistent memory, or notice how a single word appears frequently. If you keep journals on a computer, you can simply do a word search and highlight entries. Going through freewriting entries about her father, a journal keeper was overwhelmed by all the stories she'd recorded. Pages and pages under "Dad." Soon she noticed that *hand* or *hands* appeared often. To shape the material, she selected four memories of her father: guiding her seven-year-old hand on an early-morning fishing trip; slipping pocket money into her hand in college; later stroking "his arthritic joints expanded inside hard, awkward hands"; in his last moments of life, "intertwining our pinkies like we always did," feeling the final "stream of energy through his hand to mine." Images of her father's hands had not only given her a clue as to how to focus and frame the entries, they also worked thematically to capture an unbroken father-daughter connection.

Sandy Khan and Patrick Morton both trace life patterns by returning to significant dreams recorded over time. Often a single dream has its own pattern, such as images of keys or doors being opened. Donna Stein started keeping journals at ten ("I asked my mother to buy me a pack of three marbled notebooks at the drugstore"). She now has more than forty. "For the last eighteen years I've focused on keeping creative notebooks and dream journals, the essential link in personal and creative life." They hold patterns she looks at specifically: "the parts that deal with my own creativity, my desire and periodic failures. I look for places where I hear my voice is strongest."

One significant image recurs in her journals: being taken as a child by her grandmother to a "beautiful indoor garden and aviary with birds and fish in St. Louis." While visiting her once-active ninety-six-year-old grandmother in a nursing home, Donna reminded her of the St. Louis bird and fish garden. "If heaven existed, I told her, that's what I suspected it would look like. 'I'll let you know,' she replied.

"Several weeks later, my husband was out of town, and my children were sleeping in sleeping bags on the floor of my bedroom. At midnight I suddenly was wakened from a vivid dream: brilliant images of plants and fish cascaded on the wallpaper. Several gold balls of light were traveling over my children in their sleeping bags and over me. The next morning, my father called to tell me my grandmother had died exactly at midnight. A year later, I used the dream as the opening of a short story that got published."

Linking the Life Patterns

To begin linking patterns, group snapshots into any of the ten journal categories, such as mastery or hidden gifts, discussed in the last chapter. The largest categories will be key moments charting conflict or confidence, or where longing still exists. Lori Peterson discovered this to be the case. In her early forties, her son in college, she was soon to enter law school. Yet success had always been shadowed by a hidden longing to know "the people who look like me. Where are they? Who are they? When I know the answers, I will know who I am." The "898th child to be adopted" from Korea, she was raised in America. Having no memory of her Korean childhood, she wrote a series of letters in her journal to her birth mother. "I am a grown woman. Recently, I've been thinking of you, wondering what you are like, and if I look like you. A loving couple who could not have loved me more had I been their biological child adopted me. From them I learned common sense, compassion, empathy for others. Yet I've missed you all my life. Have you, me?" The letters allowed her to put her longing to work: doing an anthology of stories about Korean-American adoptees, lifting "the shroud of silence" of a transplanted childhood.

Supplying the missing links in a life was the reason Cathryn Griffith began a family chronicle for her twenty-one-year-old daughter, Sarah. One family story had overshadowed everything, circumstances Cathy recorded only tersely in occasional journals: that she, her husband, and mother had all had cancer the same year. Cathy's mother had died when Sarah was two. Then her husband. Then she herself took sick. At midlife, she recalls, "Although I was an adult, I felt orphaned as well as widowed. The entire universe had changed for me. My touchstones were gone."

While she'd taped family photos low to the ground so her young daughter would recognize faces, Cathy wanted to leave a fuller story for Sarah; "one not of loss, but of continuity." Sifting through generations of material in her mind, she began with a single memory. On the first page of her chronicle she writes, "I remember walking out the kitchen door to go to my husband's funeral and realizing at that moment that I must find within myself the courage and wisdom and energy to create a new family life for myself and my daughter. Memories sustained me. I drew on my reserve of love and wisdom and spent a lot of time just trying to figure things out. Photographs and stories guided me in giving my daughter a sense of her personal history."

That history reached back generations. The photographs and stories supplied far more than a social history — family leaving England in 1630; crossing the frontier; mining in the gold rush. The material supplied deeper missing patterns. The first: that from the 1860s, family history had been "recorded, gathered and passed from mother to daughter." As she sifted documents,

Cathy saw bold patterns mirroring her own life: on her mother's side, each woman was widowed early; each assumed a husband's business; each was a success. Playfully, she uses the earliest family tree as a graphics backdrop, showing how females were single forgotten lines.

The final chronicle format highlights life's strange connections and coincidences. Next to blocks of family history (ancestors first settling in Cambridge, Massachusetts, for example), Cathy juxtaposes an italicized pattern from her own life. How in her twenties, "ignorant of my family's history," she was "living a quarter of a mile from the place where my immigrant ancestors had lived 330 years earlier." A rich visual and narrative tapestry, the finished chronicle is a tiny foldout book whose accordion pages zigzag like the lives inside. Visual imagery — ships, wagons, cars — offers a shorthand of centuries of change; sailboats connect Cathy's husband, herself, and her daughter.

Her mother's finished chronicle was partly responsible for Sarah's decision to go to graduate school in book preservation. Reading her great-great-grandmother's diary written from 1868 to 1925, she saw how its patterns foreshadowed the strengths of three generations of women in the family: (vocation) 1868 (age 20): "I wonder what my life work is to be"; (leaving a family record) 1879 (age 31): "I would like to write a

150

journal that my children could own and be benefited by if I were taken away. If I were to leave them now, what would they ever know about me?"; (zeal for life) 1905 (age 58): "The Bible says there's a time to dance. If so, now is mine."

Focusing and Shaping Material

Museum consultant Lallie Lloyd began journals in her thirties as "creative and spiritual dialogues. Each involves the making of meaning. Diaries are the self's first drafts. They have to sit often before a final meaning surfaces in our lives." When I met her, she was struggling to focus a sprawling family chronicle. Whose story to tell first? How to find and narrow the focus? Instead of starting with old journals, I suggested she first do three narrative snapshots — object, place, single incident — from her *own* life to unlock stories hidden within facts. She did a snapshot a week. But even before she began lining them up, clues and patterns had emerged in the first one. For the object snapshot, she'd chosen something she thought odd at the time: a carved head of an angel, "brown, once-living wood now seamed by years and smoothed by touch." It had sat on her minister husband's desk "full of tokens and books," rarely glanced at.

As she sat down, she assumed it would trigger the story of their marriage: how she'd met Scott at nineteen while both were students at Yale, how they'd married after graduation, and had two children in close succession. Yet two completely different stories surfaced as she began to write. The first explored his recent unexpected death while out of town on a trip. The second involved someone else's story, which started to dominate the narrative. "It doesn't really look like her at all," Lallie wrote of the carved head. The mysterious "she" emerged fully only when Lallie did the single-incident exercise. It was her three-year-old sister, Muffy, a persistent but long-hidden memory. At five, her parents away, Lallie accompanied the housekeeper and two neighborhood children on a drive. Muffy was in back of the housekeeper's car. Then Lallie heard the strange click of a door unlocking. Decades later, the ride remained a picture "caught in two dimensions, cropped and still" in memory: "tall trees in their gray January bareness, a small blond child lay on her back on the road, not moving, bundled in her winter coat, red leather sandals on her feet."

Her sister's accidental death was rarely spoken of at home. "My mother told me my little sister would be my guardian angel. Lucky me. For who can turn alone?" The place snapshot had included a haunting image

152

from a dream Lallie had at twelve, but never recorded in a journal. "I carried her across the sunlit back porch toward the warmth and welcome of the kitchen. The porch was glassed-in on one side and the other wall had a long shelf where the milkman left bottles of milk." In the dream, trying to navigate around tight corners, "I could have steered better, but I didn't quite clear the corner, so one of her legs gently bumped against the shelf. She exploded in my arms."

The simple wooden object had unearthed subconscious meaning: her sister, and later her husband, had been the first of a series of "earth angels" in Lallie's life. They were people who had shown her how to "risk life and love again" after their loss. That thematic pattern became a way to organize the material. As she lined up the snapshots, she saw others who figured in that story: her mother and a favorite, gifted cousin. The writing produced an immediate result. Lallie went back to talk to the two childhood friends who had been in the car that January day. No one had ever talked to them about Muffy's death. Lallie discovered that for over thirty years each had mistakenly felt responsible for the accident.

The conversations helped heal their guilt as survivors. On her way home, Lallie also realized that finally writing openly about her husband's sudden death had also healed her own guilt (the couple had been separated at the time). The narrative snapshots focused what was still submerged in years of journals. In a second round, she wrote only single-incident scenes, zeroing in on every ten years of family life. By focusing on key moments, she saw the life lessons just under the surface of the losses: "how important having children has been for me; my love of children in general; my unshakable belief in speaking up in life, no matter how late." In her forties, she now knows the importance of not just leaving a trace, but a true one.

"What surprised me is how in telling others' stories, I also began to leave a portrait of myself. How I'd struggled to finally find meaning beyond loss. And how that too is a deep form of creativity." To remind her, the carved wooden figure "hangs on the wall next to where I sit mornings." As she continues exploring the stories of the lives it reminds her of, "they hold me up, breathe for me."

Finding Missing Links

Unlike Lallie Lloyd, Ray Zager followed a straight chronology when writing about an important segment of his life: being a solider in World War II. What could be simpler than consulting events recorded in all those indexed journals? It was all there: arriving in France in 1945, first as part of the U.S. Seventy-first Infantry Division; fighting to the Rhine River; transferring to General Patton's Third Army. Yet a key life moment was missing. It didn't surface until 1988. While purchasing the published diary of a fifteen-year-old Lithuanian boy, Yitshok Rudasheuski, at the Ghetto Fighter's Museum in Israel, Zager saw a museum map "showing the camps including Gunskichen Lager." The very sight of the camp's name reminded Ray Zager why his story was different from thousands of American soldiers.

Ray had been a motor messenger, "driving between frontline companies, battalions, and regiments." On a moonless April night on the Austrian border, Zager got his first glimpse of the horrors of "Mr. War God" amid the muddy fields. As dawn broke and his battalion was radioed, "I couldn't put into words what I was seeing. Only a God of War could do that." Zager, one of two American Jewish soldiers in his company, had come to the Gunskichen Lager concentration camp as the Germans were fleeing.

Decades later, coming across a fifteen-year-old boy's published diary, Zager finally set down his own memories. Aware that "in Rudasheuski's diary those lives cut short live on in a book," Zager dedicated his

memoir to the memory of those in the camp, while
continuing to dedicate each of his own journals to
his immediate family. While Volume 36, 1987, for
example, covers "my retirement, which shall give me
more time to study, work, and write," it's full of family
life. "Because I feel so strongly about the value of the
diary, I want another's good name, or another's ideas, or
whatever is good in the world to be honored by dedi-
cating my writing to my wife and children."

As so many of the journal keepers in this chapter
discovered, stories wait months, often years, before
being told. They wait until we're ready to tell them.
Beginning to know where to look for them, as Andre
Gide said of his famous diaries, is "the silent waiting
that precedes good work." Then, as Virginia Woolf
noted, "It is in our idleness, in our dreams, that the submerged truth comes to the top."

EXERCISES AND JOURNAL PROMPTS

༺ Begin indexing a new journal. The ideal way is to
   start with one that's only halfway through. Do five
   to ten pages a sitting. Using different color highlighter pens, use one color for each type of entry:
   events, other people, reflections. If you keep journals on a computer, print major index entries on

different colored paper. Yellow, for example, for creative work. Blue for dreams. Green for reflections. They can be kept in separate thematic binders.

∽ Once you've lined up four or more entries, make a list of recurring images or words. Notice if a thematic pattern links them. If not, take five minutes to freewrite on associations the image or word triggers. Connections will appear almost instantly, showing ways to begin seeing the entries or snapshots in a new organizational light.

∽ To frame stories covering a series of years, pick a single key life pattern (confidence, conflict, hidden lessons, etc.). Write a short paragraph showing yourself (or another) at important ages: ten, seventeen, twenty-one, thirty, forty, sixty-five. Since most journal entries are first done in summary, expanding description into even mini paragraph snapshots will frame and link material. Begin keeping separate journals or binders for each key life pattern. In time, the snapshots will reel like a film.

CHAPTER VIII

Transforming the Stories: Seeing Anew

∽

*Having to stare . . . not getting the point at once. The
longer you look at one object, the more of the world you
see in it.*

— FLANNERY O'CONNOR

THAT SNOWY AFTERNOON I stayed home with a cold a
lot happened. I was simply sitting on a bed, surrounded
by stacks of odd-sized notebooks and crumpled
Kleenex, but an hour into reading old journals, I knew
that far more than a carton had been opened. Whole
worlds had reemerged: forgotten names, faces, places.
I found things I wanted to remember; other things I
didn't. Amid it all, the journals offered a way of seeing
anew. Completely anew. I saw how moods I'd once jot-

ted with such anxious precision had been as shifting and fickle as the New England weather outside. Entries were often exaggerated. Plain wrong or missing the point other times. The point was all the material that lay under the writing: fragments of stories or deeper memory that needed to coalesce into new meaning.

No matter what anybody tells you, rereading an old journal the first time through is like a thrillingly cheap novel. You read for the dramas, the dirt, the sanctimonious comfort of having set the record straight. Or did you? After only a few pages, I quickly scanned past complaints and vapory moods to solid islands of fact or description. I hungered for the few scenes I'd made vivid, for portraits of others, not just of myself. But I discovered that even the portraits needed to be seen again, over and over, before a fuller truth about a life, a scene, a turning point becomes clear.

After all, hadn't I kept a commonplace book to remind me of just that? Passages or quotes copied from others' diaries help keep things in perspective. Short story writer John Cheever, for example, in quiet despair as he turned forty, "without having accomplished any one of the things I intended to accomplish — without ever having achieved the deep creativity that I have worked toward all this time." He castigated himself for not being talented. "It is not that these are stories of failure; that is not what is frightening. It is that they are dull annals; they are of no import . . . of no importance to anyone." Only years later would Cheever go back to his journal and see that he was in fact working on some of his most important stories for *The New Yorker*.

My commonplace book was full of headings I'd noted to remind me how self-selecting memory is, how it often clouds self-perception the first time. Amid headings for writers on bad moods, fears, or confidence, I also had a "solutions" category. How Virginia Woolf, for example, reread her diary at the end of each year to confirm that being sick or depressed hadn't prevented her from creating a new novel. Instead she saw yearlong patterns of resourcefulness, using or working against self-doubt. To remind herself, she often began a new entry with "For future reference," helping her to cast aside ups and downs of daily life. Or as Gail Godwin says of her diaries, "I write for my future self, as well as my present mood. And sometimes, to set the record straight, I jot down a word or two in old diaries to my former self — to encourage, to scold, to correct, to set things in perspective."

On that snowy afternoon I realized I needed ways to expand and comment on old journals. I'd already found one solution — keeping a current journal quickly written at the moment; another, often started years later, that consisted simply of single-incident snapshots for key times or turning points in a life. The second journal fleshed out or framed stories only hinted at in the original. That journal, as poet Henri Cole notes, tapped "the mind in repose, the heart excavating itself."

But I didn't want to wait until seized with another cold before learning ways to reframe entries, to see new patterns or stories. That afternoon I'd noticed that all journals, not just mine, have at least three through lines that unify the earlier mentioned pattern categories, ongoing questions involving ambition, decisions, memory. Or, put another way, ways to identify the roots of longing and action. Look hard at entries that focus on unresolved childhood fears, especially loss. Observe where entries reveal how often you use crisis to fuel determination and how doing so has shaped who you are today. To follow any of these strands in a journal is to uncover its linked stories. What is it I still long for? What first created the longing? How has it shaped my life over the years?

These were questions I needed to ask as I read the stack's last two journals, a spiral notebook and a tiny journal, both largely about my father. In the last year and a half of his life, I'd completely reseen him and our relationship. My new journals hadn't recorded the consequences of that shift. But the old journals, I now saw

161

clearly, were full of longing for that shift to happen. Soon after rereading those two earlier journals, I began to craft stories.

Seeing Again: Revising a Life

The pleasure and freedom of journals is that they're written on the pulse — lightning-quick notations that don't care about wording or style. To keep a journal is to know the present is still under consideration, merely a first draft of your experience. Going through old journals offers a chance to step back from the stories we tell ourselves, separating fact from emotion, to create another, more complete draft. What had once been tragic in a diary is later clearer, often revelatory, a source of self-knowledge.

Revision literally means "to see again." That's exactly what Anne Frank did. In May 1944, she began to revise her entire diary. "I have one outstanding trait," she wrote, "and that is knowledge of myself. I can watch myself and my actions, just like an outsider." With an eye to turning her diary into a book published after the war, she revised entries, compressing scenes, inventing pseudonyms to free herself to write about others. Diaries, she knew, were all about reseeing, about lining up the life. "You need bits of the world to toss around," says Annie Dillard. "You start anywhere, and join the bits into a pattern by your writing about them."

As my cold dragged on that weekend, I played with quick ways to reframe material in old journals. I selected a key passage or entry and retyped it, especially if the original was handwritten. The very act of recopying even a single page opens up associations, reframing perspective. In a journal, you can paste the old entry on the left side; the new on the right. The contrast is often dramatic — an overlay of new life patterns.

Ask what — or who — is missing. In his late forties, Bill Bassett filled in an episode missing from his college journals: a roommate who'd been murdered. Years later the loss of his friend also provided "a wild-card portrait of the counterculture sixties era." He began each new entry by finding "the wild-card" event or association memory had hidden for decades. Bassett now saw the ironies — how being a good student then had made him unpopular, but ultimately saved him; how his popular friend was killed the weekend of Woodstock; how the still-unsolved murder was in a neighborhood where he'd gone not for drugs but to tutor inner-city kids.

A vase bought for a friend's wedding but kept for herself was a memory a Boston diarist found briefly noted in an old journal. In a new journal she reflected on the years she'd known the couple. Like the vase, all their lives "had suffered cracks." Weeks later, that metaphor sparked a fuller snapshot with an even deeper metaphor: how her friendship with the wife had been the glue in all their lives. The women's solid friendship became a way to frame narrating a series of life events — shaky marriages, demanding jobs, problems with teenage kids. Similarly, someone who found all the letters she'd written from college, which her mother had saved, began a new journal reflecting not just on the omissions, but the striking difference between her public and private voices. Why in letters did she need to charm or please so much? Was she doing the same in the journals, hiding from herself?

To help her see life from two perspectives, book binder Sandy Khan created a specially bound journal. Her "Day/Night" journal is written on opposite ends. Starting on the Night side (with its own moon cover), she records dreams. She flips to the opposite Day side for morning pages, reflecting on a dream's meaning, helping her illuminate desires and conscious life choices. "My conscious and subconscious meet in the same journal." Literary agent Sally Brady reframes old entries by imagining new solutions. Whenever she's stumped by how to solve a problem (often one about creative work), she uses guided imagery. It may be bringing something important on a journey, for example. "I reread an entry and visualize myself now being provided with a key, for example. Locked doors open."

Transformation: Finding the Thread

In 1975, writer Annie Dillard was living in a small cabin in Puget Sound, Washington. Having just turned thirty, she wondered: "What was my life about? Why was I living alone, when I am gregarious?" After winning the Pulitzer Prize for *Pilgrim at Tinker Creek* (written partly in the form of an essayistic nature journal), she was having a hard time writing except in journals. One of them, though, contained two entries that would spark her now famous essay "Transfiguration." The process of writing the essay from those journals deepened her commitment to her vocation as a writer.

Embedded in her journal was an incident she'd witnessed one night in her cabin: a moth burning steadily in a candle. It was a persistent memory that became a clue to unlocking deeper patterns. "I went to my pile of journals, hoping I'd taken some nice specific notes." What she found disappointed her — long descriptions of owl sounds. The next night's entry, though, "after pages of self-indulgent drivel," held a fuller description. "The journal entry had some details I could use

165

(bristleworms on the ground, burnt moths' wings sticking to pans), some phrases (her body acted like a wick, the candle had 2 flames, the moth burned until I blew it out), and, especially, some verbs (hiss, recoil, stick, spatter, jerked, crackled)."

She began her detective work, uncovering what the emerging essay was really about. Why had she made the moth a female? It triggered a deeper memory of being on a camping trip at sixteen, reading a book about the inspired but self-destructive French poet Rimbaud. How did the moth, the poet, the memory all figure in Dillard's present life? "With my old journal beside me, I took up my current journal and scribbled and doodled my way through an account of my present life and the remembered moth."

A larger portrait slowly emerged. She remembered how when reading about Rimbaud at sixteen, moths had also burned in the camp light. So, she recalled, had her love of writing that night. Memory and meaning began to fuse. The poet and the moth both burned with light. So, Dillard realized, would she again. At thirty she knew that a writer, once inspired, is a luminous channel for work. The old journal had rekindled her. As the essay wove itself from journal notes, it held images that would guide all her future work: how the poet, the mystic, even the martyr use "materials of the world" to transform it.

Life Is in the Details: Defining Images

Virginia Woolf called them "shivering fragments," those rich clues the mind leaves in journals as it first records the world. I call them tension points. My students call them hot spots. Whatever the phrase, they're where the eye zooms in and stays fixed. Where you think: *yes*, this is the journal's truest part. Like Dillard's burning moth, they're encoded with our life stories. "We only store in memory images of value," says Patricia Hampl. The task in rereading is "stalking the relationship, seeking the congruence between stored image and hidden emotion." Culling past journals, you train the eye to see and record stronger details in future pages. The proof is in a sharpened observing world journal, which thickens with fine details. To stare at them anew is to find ways to unlock the stories that still need telling.

For Angela Densted, memory is "a tone that reverberates." She returns to old journals "when the echoing is persistent, knowing stories are ready to be written." She recently reread journals to clarify stories about two childhood worlds. Now, with a cool eye, she no longer judges a hardscrabble childhood spent with a loving mother. The stories that wanted telling were of memories of the Minnesota farm where she visited her father only two weeks a year. Until now, that story always got lost in writing about the family's complexity — her parents' divorce, inheriting three stepmothers and many half siblings. To find the deeper stories, she focused only on "details that shimmer." Usually they were quirky, vivid, unsettling. She'd already transcribed key journal passages onto a computer. She then highlighted details in italics to see their patterns.

Among them: "the free clinic where they'd prick my finger every week and exchange my blood for food"; "the jumper that ended somewhere above my knees, leaving a gap of skinny joints showing before the white of my knee socks"; "the quick camouflaged movements of deer; farm fields turned to gold, but it was a gold I could run through, pluck, put in my hair." Memories surfaced of the farmhouse with "carved wooden loons in phosphorescent paint"; "velvet Elvis and John Wayne portraits next to the gun rack"; "the elaborate dragon-shaped candle that never got burned." Among it all, she recalled the father who'd left when she was four, away in Vietnam and the Grand Tetons. "All Dad had taken from my life was the baby tooth he pulled out, leaving that strange space and the taste of blood in my mouth. He had dropped the tooth in a flask of ocean water from Florida, left behind when he left us."

Finally she found the detail that triggered all the stories: "That Christmas had been the only time I'd ever felt sorry for my father's second wife. I knew before she did that the marriage was over." Remembering the most recent Christmas, she used a series of flashbacks of other Christmases as contrast to tell a twenty-five-year story. It was all in there: a father, a tough-fragile man she'd long loved but never known well. A father proud but wary of his now adult daughter. Here's her new opening:

I can picture him as he was last Christmas morning, bare-chested, toothless, aiming his .22 Baretta out the bedroom window. He hadn't seen me in six months, but still no use in missing a shot. He gave me a quick glance, smiling wide so I'd be sure to notice his top teeth were gone. "Had 'em out last Thursday," he said, his sunken smile the shape of a half-moon eclipsed by his red beard. "I wanted to heal up before I go back to work. Most people they put under. Not me." He lined up the bead with his target. "Just a couple of shots of novocaine." He squeezed the trigger. He was killing blue jays for stealing food from the smaller birds his third wife likes to feed. If there's one thing he can't stand, it's a bully.

169

"Well?" he said, looking at me. I shrugged my shoulders, shuffling in my stocking feet, and stammered the only phrase I could think to say. "Merry Christmas, Dad."

The Slowly Emerging Self-Portrait

Often it's easier to see shifts or life patterns in someone else's journals. (A notorious case was that of nineteenth-century British physician Dr. Palmer. Noticing inconsistencies in his journal, police realized he'd poisoned his wife.) Initially, what prevents us from seeing our own journals clearly isn't its lies or omissions. It's the habitual way we tell stories or choose to present ourselves. We do it daily. At diners, over coffee, we tell the same stories about ourselves the same way: with a kind of hypnotic consistency. The telling is as reflexive as a résumé.

Tom Brown's résumé is worth repeating. A space exploration engineer, he's contributed to the Jupiter *Galileo* and Saturn *Cassini* spacecrafts. At fifty, he wrote in a journal, "I like analogies. They let me see things from different angles. For instance, take life as an arrangement of glass panels in a black room. A person is a light beam that travels about the room through various panels, leaving the room a little warmer. Each glass panel is an event that can focus, diffuse, filter or even amplify a light beam hitting it."

A central event in his life was a college dorm prank that literally exploded in his face. With a fellow chemical engineer, he performed an experiment that sent lye and glass shards into his eye, scarring his cornea, leaving him partially blind. "My wavy clear vision clouded to translucent white." Thirty-five years later, he traced the real stories hidden in a series of journal entries. Earlier notations, understandably, had focused on loss: the eighteen-month recovery, a scrapped medical career. Rereading his entries, he now saw how the accident "in a blink of an eye, deflected and focused me in a new direction." Learning Braille, he'd finished his Ph.D., married, and had children.

But as he reframed entries, a deeper pattern emerged. "For nineteen years I was a semi-innocent bystander in my own life, trying to follow a path I thought someone else had set out for me." He now resaw his childhood in a pinched, rigid Utah family in a new light. "I emerged from a black wall in 1944, as an unexpected gleam in my parents' eye, no focus or plan." Told he'd never do anything special in life, he saw the accident as a hard but hidden gift. Near blindness had defined and galvanized him. To link his stories, he used the journal's many metaphors of eyes and light to arrive at his final meaning: how he'd traded loss of his sight for insight into his own character, something he explores now, writing about family or even about his gift of being an accomplished glass maker.

Journals as Double Portraits

If every journal is a self-portrait, it's also a gallery of other portraits. (Remember how impossible it was to keep the place-prompt just about you; others kept showing up.) In those two journals I found on that snowy afternoon my father appears constantly. One contained endless lists of details; the other, a series of single-paragraph snapshots. Years earlier, the journals had given me practical ways to fill time — and cope — as my father went in and out of consciousness as I sat next to him the final weeks of his life.

The journals then sat for six years. Glad I'd kept them at the time, I hadn't looked at them again until recently. I'd been asked to write something for an anthology about writers and their fathers. It was one of those nightmarish open-ended topics. The editor, offering a kind of diary prompt, suggested I try it as a letter, opening with "I've always meant to tell you." I was stumped. So I sat down and did what I tell my classes to do when stumped: start first with an object.

I knew instantly what to choose. I knew just where to find it. Sure enough, the first journal had precise details about the radiation film. My father, looking remarkably fit, had handed it to me right after he'd been diagnosed. It was among the final photographs of him. And now dozens of details I hadn't recalled since first recording them came to life.

"In rows of three, the thick film framed a dozen tiny standing images of you. Back to front. Hands fanning your sides. I studied the exposed X-ray white of your body, staring where the cancer left dark asterisks. In your pelvis, two symmetrical images. Flowers or dust. They shimmered like stars.

"In the second contact sheet, two months later, your whole body was now dotted with a spray of dark confetti.

"Holding the contact sheet, I marveled at how it had managed the impossible: trapping you. The father always traveling, always gone — even when sitting near me in the living room, the secret thrill of the outside world a smell on your skin. How was it possible that in the MRI images you were only three inches square?"

The object gave me a way to structure the essay: using each film image as a small window revealing a story about my father. (The stories had originally been jotted in the second snapshot journal.) The stories had a pattern: a father there, not there. Using the photo-that-never-existed prompt, I then created a parallel series of new images: the silent ways he *had* been there; how, like the magician he'd hired for my sixth-grade birthday party, his illness gave us strange new ways of seeing the other.

But I still didn't know how to open the piece. It wasn't the whole story. I needed to capture the paradox of this final reseeing. The missing link, a memory never recorded in a journal, surfaced as I struggled with the essay's first draft. I suddenly recalled how a friend in college had once asked me when my father had died. Horrified, I'd replied that he was still very much alive. Why did she think he wasn't? I spoke of him rarely, she said, and "always in the past tense." That all changed by the time he really died years later. By then we were fully present tense, father and daughter, stubbornly alike. But it would take looking for tension-point details in old journals to let me know how true that had always been.

A confession: the portrait still isn't right. While it's soon to be published, there's something still not true at the core. As a portrait it's still too protective of my father, lacking in final complex shading. That essay was just a first draft of emotion. I'd written it out of love —

but also as if afraid he could still read and judge it. But there was a deeper issue. I couldn't write about my father, I knew, without writing about myself. To unlock his story was somehow to unlock mine as well. For now, that's sent me back to writing about why I saved certain objects of his. One is a journal I'd given him after he retired so he might record his life. After his death, I found it. Still blank.

In a new notebook I'll be revising that portrait, trying to see it more clearly. In the meantime, the original journals sit, details thickening, waiting, as I write this sentence instead.

EXERCISES AND JOURNAL PROMPTS

∽ Trace one of the three hidden narrative strands (ambition, patterns of action around longing, earliest memories of either) in a single journal. After highlighting with a different color pen, or recopying entries, list the deeper stories hidden in each entry. Explore a story a week.

∽ Use guided imagery to tackle solving what's still unsaid in an old journal entry. Imagine a box left next to your journal. It holds a number of items you've lost. Each will help solve a problem recorded in a past journal. Without letting the pen lift, quickly describe what's in the box. Pick one item and freewrite half a page, seeing the situation anew.

∽ To reframe material, imagine a past situation as a photograph rather than a journal entry. Introduce a single element that could alter the photo. A new mother, for example, imagining having an extra hour to herself. Or the consequences of staying in a marriage.

∽ Do a cluster drawing tiered like a bunch of grapes. Think of something you'd like reframed. At the bottom, in a single grape, describe the situation as you see it. At the next level up, what three close friends would see; at the top, complete strangers' perspective.

∽ Take a single journal entry. Imagine if this were written by your spouse or child. What would you tell them is the hidden lesson, the hidden gift they hadn't seen?

∽ Twice a month, take an old complaining entry. Line it up with a new entry showing a shift or break-through, however small.

∽ Once a week write a journal entry in the third person to give yourself instant distance and perspective.

PART THREE

CROSSOVER
Moving a Journal into Creative Work

*Two or three things I know for sure;
and one of them is what it means to
have no loved version of your life but
the one you make.*

—Dorothy Allison

CHAPTER IX

Finding the Through Line in a Life: Memoir and Fiction

To write about one's life is to live it twice, and the second living is both spiritual and historical, for a memoir reaches deep within the personality as it seeks its narrative form.

—Patricia Hampl

THE LETTER OPENS like this:

> This is the first mention — the first seed — of the short story in my journal. It came, as many of my stories do, as a list. I was working as a pet sitter. The previous evening I'd been in the apartment of a woman I'd never met (my boss did the client interviews, then gave us the keys, sending us on our way). I was there to take care of

her parrot. It had snowed the day before, a deep snow. I stood at the kitchen window of her apartment, then turned to open the freezer door to get peanuts for the parrot. The refrigerator was an ancient thing — I'd had a similar one once, a pain to defrost. Sure enough, inside the freezer was coated with three inches of ice. The peanuts, a package of peas and a bottle of tequila were embedded within.

An image came into my head of a woman sitting in this kitchen in the heat of summer, drinking Coronas and tequila with a friend, waiting for the freezer to defrost. A parrot nearby. The next morning when I was freewriting in my journal, the image came up again. It was followed by other images. I had no idea how they connected at the time, but I had a feeling there was a story there.

There was. Cindy Riede had just sent it to me, the soon-to-be-published short story "Darwin's Kitchen." It was attached almost as an afterthought to other material — pages photocopied from her spiral notebook journal. They chart the progression of the story: lists, questions, first drafts, revisions. She'd sent along the journal notes, including one entry about a shopping list she'd once found on the street. Tucked away in her journal, it later inspired a character portrait of the person who'd lost the list.

But as I read the first reply of how her journal holds story images, I found myself equally caught up by something else. It was the story of *her* — the pet sitter in that apartment — that I found so quirky and lively. It felt like part of a memoir or novel I'd love to read: the itinerant life of someone who wants to write, but who takes odd jobs in the meantime, jobs she's detailed and stored as future material in her nearly forty journals.

Journals contain the plot of our lives. Yet until we begin looking with new eyes, we often miss how interesting the material is. Others see it, though. Ask anyone who's ever picked up a journal at a book fair or auction. Like novels, diaries offer us an insider's view of other worlds or eras. (Recently, a journal similar to my grandmother's — kept during war relief work in World War One Russia — fetched $1,900 at a book auction.) We read them for clues to a specific life, to see what it is like to see with another's eyes. Otto Klemperer's recently published diaries (excerpted in *The New Yorker*) detail first seeing a child's ball or toothpaste tube emblazoned with a swastika. Civil War diaries document not just an individual's unique fate but a nation's.

Diaries are the ideal preparation for the sea change of moving into memoir. A journal is the first draft of experience; revision gives a diarist a sense of control in shaping a life's story, supplying context, imagining an audience beyond oneself. "True memoir," says Patricia Hampl, "is written in an attempt to find not only a self but a world."

That is just what long-term journal keepers do who want to transform material into creative work: move from notes to narrative, from private to public voice. They first start with forms of autobiographical writing to see what genre — memoir, fiction, poetry — they ultimately want to stay with. Creative nonfiction uses the facts of a life, the techniques of fiction, and the resonant imagery of poetry.

Over the years, either as a writer in residence or in creative nonfiction workshops, I have shown people how in even a single afternoon they can shift into a deeper creative voice. Five of the earlier snapshot prompts, used in quick succession, serve as building blocks of storytelling. Each, in turn, taps fresh writing skills. The object prompt yields concrete powers of description; place involves writing from the senses, thereby evoking sensory details. With the single incident, you began to frame narrative and locate story conflict. The character portrait and missing photo prompt supply deeper story layers in any life.

Unlocking the Story

When Lisa Colt looks at all her journals "stacked in the laundry room bookcase, their spines numbered chronologically in white ink," she knows they "connect the dots" of her story. How to shape the plot of one's life? Autobiography is the chronological telling of one's life. It's usually unedited, a blow-by-blow account of pertinent facts: birth, family, education, marriage, career. In a sense, it's closest to a first go at a diary — full of surface information. That information, still unfiltered, is almost a straight transcription of events.

Memoir, by contrast, selects from key facts an angle it wants to concentrate on: exploring a specific aspect of childhood or family life. Memoir often highlights a narrower time range. Unlike autobiography, memoir focuses on *solving a question,* usually about identity, which in turn reveals a narrative line of beginning, middle, and end. Maya Angelou's still bestselling memoir *I Know Why the Caged Bird Sings* focuses on the first sixteen years of her life. Susanna Kaysen's *Girl, Interrupted* deals with just two years in a life remembered twenty years later. Their enduring success lies in showing a particular life story that also strikes a universal chord. Both memoirs could have stayed stashed away as material in journals. But each shows what memoir does

at its best: it gives others courage — and permission —
to unlock similar stories still hidden in journals.

The Portrait in the Mirror

All genres — fiction, memoir, poetry — involve some
form of self-portrait. But how to separate your stories
from others' lives; how to claim that *I?* To begin to
move from a journal into creative narrative, whether
fiction or memoir, here are some questions to ask:
What's at stake for the protagonist? (In this case, oneself
in the journal.) Risking losing love? Settling for a comfortable but still not happy life? *What are the obstacles
that hinder or define character along the way? What, in
retrospect, was the hidden key or gift that turned things
around?* (Often it's humor. One of my favorite memoirs
is Tobias Wolff's *This Boy's Life,* chronicling his haphazard childhood with a difficult stepfather. It's Wolff's
subversive intelligence, humor, and, ultimately, help
from his older brother on the East Coast that saved
him.)

Finding the Through Line

Unconsciously, in journal keeping one tries to find the
arc of a life's meaning. I call it the through line, a phrase

borrowed from screenwriters. It is possible to find it once you've reread old journals, located key patterns, reframed stories. With any current journal, imagine yourself in the third, not first, person. Then ask yourself: What does the protagonist want most? Fill in the blank with a "to" statement: "to find a home," for example, "to be forgiven," "to define success on one's own terms." This creates a larger thematic frame, which will automatically select related journal material.

A helpful way to define the deeper self-portrait that's at the core of memoir is to ask: If this were a novel, what are two endings — the old familiar one or a newly imagined one? This often dramatically affects the life as well as the work. In her late thirties, Alison Frank is a research scientist who grew up in Spain and was educated in America. When Alison was in her late twenties, her mother had stolen her old boyfriend while visiting him in Spain. Years later, after learning of the brief affair, Alison resaw her years of caretaking a brilliant but distant mother. She decided to create a through line in her journal, "to assume control, not be controlled" by others. In doing so, her relationship with her mother had a whole new ending.

Shaping the Story with Details

The most important shift when first moving from journals into memoir is the selection process. Knowing which details or stories to *omit* is as important as what to pick. "The writer of memoir," says William Zinsser, "must become the editor of his own life. He must prune an unwieldy story and give it narrative shape." To do so, look for diary passages where you've told the life story factually; see if you can now let specific details <u>show</u> the story instead, evoking it in a series of narrative snapshots. In memoir, each detail serves to shape the story's mood or final point.

To help focus that final point ask yourself: *What do you want the reader to feel by the end of the memoir?* In her autobiographical essay "Goodbye to All That," Joan Didion shows how her naïve optimism at twenty-one masked not assuming responsibility for adult life. "It is easy to see the beginnings of things, and harder to see the ends" opens the essay on her eight uncommitted years in New York. She lets carefully selected details show it — living in an apartment with only a borrowed bed, two French garden chairs, and fifty yards of theatrical silk for curtains that tangle in the rain. Even details in the first few paragraphs hint at something already awry: the dress that felt so chic in Sacramento suddenly seems dowdy and wrong as she arrives in New York. The air smells of mildew. Staying in a hotel and not knowing how to tip, she catches a horrible cold because she's too terrified to call for someone to turn off the air-conditioning.

Novelist, poet, and essayist Phillip Lopate has long raided his earlier journals for similarly rich finds. "I was like a squirrel hiding away nuts for an older me who would raid the stash." That stash, increasingly, went into his autobiographical and nonfiction writing. "I have found there to be a more intimate, direct connection between journal-writing and personal essay-writing than any work I had previously done in other genres." Even before putting together his definitive *The Art of the Personal Essay*, Lopate found that insights in a journal often waited to be used "as a springboard" into later autobiographical writing.

Writing About the World

When you shift from journals to memoir, you have to supply context for a reader. No matter what your subject, you're always writing about a specific place, culture, even historical era. A decade after a trip, Melinda Papowitz reread extensive travel journals she'd kept as a student visiting India, Pakistan, and Israel. She now saw each country in a new light. The journals were packed with vivid details: markets where traveling *fakirs,* Islamic folk doctors, in white shirts and green turbans sold drugged lizards thought to cure impotence. Merchants sold "cheap clay saucers, rolled up socks, heaps of stiff bras. Palm readers had their booths; a parrot pecked a playing card that revealed the future." Outside a nearby saint's shrine, "pilgrims passed out rice to the poor, who sat with copper bowls between their legs."

In beginning to reframe journal entries into memoir, she noticed that, all her life, "churches, Buddhist shrines, Native American sweat lodges were my favorite destinations." A deeper pattern — her own spiritual quest — emerged in the travel journals. In seeking other religions, she saw how each tradition had slowly reconnected her to her own religious roots. "In the shadow of the Holocaust, my parents insisted on the unity of humanity. As a seeker interested in finding beauty in all religions, for me Pakistan was a testing ground. What would it be like to pause every four hours to assert God's power? To find stillness on a bedroom floor?"

To shape material, she evoked how "steamy, sinuous days in the city of Lahore, lazy as summer lemonade afternoons back home, were parceled between five calls to prayer." Watching *salat* prayers on Lahore's side streets or in gardens, she began remembering stories about her own mother's devout family. As sari-clad mourners chanted at a funeral pyre, she recalled the sounds of prayer at her Orthodox grandfather's funeral service in Brooklyn. With the journal notes helping her to shift into memoir, her imagination was free to move between two geographies: the foreign worlds that first opened the terrain of her own deeper material.

Translating worlds is something M. Elaine Mar has done from childhood. Arriving in America at age four from Hong Kong, she grew up in a working-class area of Detroit, where her family ran a restaurant. While no one in her family kept journals, she did so from age ten well through her years at Harvard. Leaving a trace, Mar told me, is for her a deep desire "to understand self in continuity, rather than in isolation." That journey is described with poetic fierceness in her memoir, *Paper Daughter*, which is as much her extended family's story as her own.

From early childhood, she was aware of translating several worlds for others.

I began almost before memory, in stages so gradual I didn't notice the shift from required Chinese calligraphy exercises to my own expression. When I was very young in Hong Kong, my mother taught me to write my family's names. My parents didn't have a lot of formal education; they came from rural China and were young during a time of war and famine. The way to keep history was to learn family names, to recite these names nightly, and to write them when paper, ink and brush were available. (And when one *could* write — literacy was an issue.)

Knowledge of these names was particularly important in the late 1880s and early 1900s, because many men from rural southern China were leaving for the U.S. under assumed names (to circumvent American immigration restrictions). Without the nightly recitations, a man's true name could be lost, forgotten to the village where he was born and where his ancestors awaited his final homecoming. My maternal grandfather was one of these men, and my mother understood her duty to remember him (and all of our ancestors). So as soon as I could hold a brush, she had me practicing calligraphy. I was no older than three, possibly as young as two.

The future memoirist, who would draw on these stories, began writing "rows upon rows of family names in Chinese calligraphy books bound with string. The pages, porous to absorb ink, were doubled so that blotting paper rested squarely between layers." During the family's second year in America, Mar's mother worried that the exercises were holding her six-year-old back in school. "My mother's solution was to have me start writing in English. She didn't care what (she couldn't read English)." Mar spent her calligraphy hour practicing English — in journals. "Along the way, the different values merged — the Chinese discipline of lettering and a more American understanding of writing as expression of emotion, content flowing to meet the lines, strokes, slashes demanded by tradition."

In high school she wrote poems in spiral notebooks; in college, bound journals for newly emerging stories. "My own writing — poetry drafts, odd lines and observations continued on notebook paper. Practice lines and scenes for narrative also showed up in the cloth-bound book. In college, I decided to stop writing because a writing instructor told me I was hopeless. I honestly thought I had stopped until I started finding bits of writing everywhere — on the windowsills and baseboards of my college dorm. When I realized what I was doing, I turned to journals in earnest."

Nearly ten years later, as she began *Paper Daughter,* "I used a lot of the images, scenes and events I'd written about in old journals. But I didn't realize this until after

I solidified the images in manuscript and on a whim reread old journals. I didn't do a straight 'lift' from the journals. I read and then reconstructed memory."

The Creative Legacy Others Pass On to Us

Exploring a story's many sides proved a breakthrough for writer Nancy Kline, deep into writing her second novel, set in the 1930s. For years, Nancy had known the family attic contained her father's war letters. But the attic in her mother's Woodstock, New York, house was "a crawl space up under the roof, unlit, insulated with bales of some substance you know you're not supposed to breathe or touch." There was no floor to speak of, "only rafters spaced two feet apart, which if you missed, would plummet you through into the house." With the temperature hovering near 100 degrees, Nancy propped "a very precarious ladder against the lip of the trapdoor opening to bring down cartons full of books and papers."

She had gone in search of her late father's war letters. What she found instead in a separate space was her mother's journal from the 1920s. "I glanced through it briefly, feeling I was trespassing," but not before finding a poem her then-single mother had written about deciding not to go through with a pregnancy. "I was astonished to come across this intimate piece of writing that my ninety-something-year-old mother had composed when she was in her mid-twenties. It was the beginning of my discovery that a person I had never met, who existed before I did, had been living in this same house my whole life; I had never met her, but here was her voice intact."

Discovering that journal and its poem, along with her mother's early voice, produced a breakthrough in Nancy's novel. Its main character is a political activist, much as her own mother had been in the 1930s. The novel's second section shifted from being "told through the daughter's eyes to through the mother's, before she was a mother. Making that discovery was as astonishing to me as a writer as discovering the poem had been to me as a daughter."

With her mother's active consent, Nancy began weaving period details from the journal into the novel, vivifying its historic setting. She'd decided the protagonist would "grow up to be a professional violinist. So I spent the next year taking lessons and talking to all the violinists I knew." Then, midway through writing the novel, Nancy discovered an entry in her mother's journal: in the 1920s, trying to find a metaphor for her political idealism, her mother had written: "An image presented itself to my mind. I was a violinist who tuned in on the broadcasting of a great symphony and played his part." As if a sign, the strange confirming coincidence made Nancy "weep for two days." She wondered if her mother's journal and its hidden material had unknowingly sparked her imagination.

While she used the quotation directly in the novel, Nancy grappled with "the boundaries" between her mother's real life and Nancy's imaginative recasting of it. After her mother thanked her in advance for "writing my biography," Nancy stumbled. "A number of times I have thought: I can't write this novel. But the thought that always follows is: You gotta." In writing fiction, "my equally demanding task as a writer has been to separate myself from the raw material as much as I can, to absorb it and then escape from it, to separate the daughter from the writer, the historical mother from the fictional mother. I want desperately to capture the authentic voice of the Thirties, and I've been given that voice. But it's got to be *my* Thirties, the Thirties filtered through my very modern eyes."

The World Reconstructed

To write about one's life is to live it twice, as Patricia Hampl says. From journals we reconstruct the world, transforming it through memory and imagination. Memoir is a journal's second draft: the world seen anew. It waits years for us in strange places. For M. Elaine Mar, it first was hidden in Chinese calligraphy books, where family names were first committed to memory, each story asking to be told. For Melinda Papowitz, the inner geography of spiritual life was hidden amid detailed but unread travel journals.

Sometimes a single sentence in a factual log releases a story. Poet Maxine Kumin recently sent me such an entry. It's from September 1995, "the year I kept a running journal about the farm, horse and garden events, woolgathering as I went along," referring to the New Hampshire farm where the Pulitzer Prize-winning poet has long resided. The log mentions "a truck full of our annual sawdust bedding" her husband unloaded in a single afternoon. "An heroic undertaking."

A year later, Kumin's poem "Chores," appeared in her collection *Connecting the Dots*. For decades, journal writing for Kumin has always been "a good habit to get into, like five-finger exercises at the piano." Often an entry has an image or memory that's stayed dormant until she brings it to life after rereading a journal. The single entry here instantly evoked the memory, transforming an ordinary event into the extraordinary — a portrait of a close marriage, the husband wondering if in the afterlife, "on the other side there's a lot less work, but just in case I'm bringing my tools."

The first three stanzas vividly evoke the scene, transforming memory into a whole new world of images.

All day he's shoveled green pine sawdust
out of the trailer truck into the chute.
From time to time he's clambered down to even
the pile. Now his hair is frosted with sawdust.
Little rivers of sawdust pour out his boots.

I hope in the afterlife there's none of this stuff
he says, stripping nude in the late September sun
while I broom off his jeans, his sweater flocked
with granules, his immersed-in-sawdust socks.
I hope there's no bedding, no stalls, no barn

no more repairs to the paddock gate the horses
burst through when snow avalanches off the roof.
Although the old broodmare, our first foal, is his,
horses, he's fond of saying, make divorces.
Fifty years married, he's safely facetious.

"One thing is sure: somewhere among the jottings there will be an image," Kumin's fellow poet and journal keeper May Sarton noted. "For me a true poem is on the way when I begin to be haunted, when it seems as if I were being asked an inescapable question." Journals long store the questions that creative work sets out to solve.

EXERCISES AND JOURNAL PROMPTS

∾ Go back in old journals, selecting ten favorite details. Weave as many of them as possible into a single narrative snapshot. Or see how many can be used as first lines for poetry.

∾ Select two entries from an old journal where you have summarized an important incident. Now try to show rather than tell that event, evoking strong concrete and sensory details.

∾ Write a one-page autobiographical statement. Do it in the third person. This immediately gives necessary distance. Then, without thinking, flip the page and list several stories left out on this factual résumé. The flip side is where to begin. It's gotten past the hypnotic, reflexive ways we choose to present ourselves.

∾ Reframe a series of old journal entries using *he* or *she* rather than *I*. It's a deceptively simple technique that defuses emotionally charged material. You can even begin early memoir drafts that way, slowly shifting to *I*.

CHAPTER X

Living to Tell the Tale: Writing About Others

❧

My first stepfather used to say that what I didn't know
would fill a book. Well, here it is.

— TOBIAS WOLFF (FROM *THIS BOY'S LIFE*)

IN 1976, novelist Ron Carlson rescued a shopping bag
his wife had mistakenly put on the curb as trash. It was
his journal. He'd just finished the first draft of his first
novel, *Betrayed by F. Scott Fitzgerald*. He dumped the
bag onto his newly cleaned desk. "My journal those
years had been a large Z.C.M.I. shopping bag which by
that August was full of half a bushel of little papers on
which I had scribbled: envelopes, folded memos, torn
slips, wedding announcements, rodeo programs and
such."

Spending the better part of that day typing up the journal's contents, he "went through this freshly typed miscellany and penciled where I thought each entry might fit into the novel." He found spots "for three quarters of my observations," gradually weaving them into the novel's second draft. "Once or twice a year when I am in need of an activity that requires no thinking, I pull this folder and type it into a computer file titled 'Notes,' which is simply a second cousin of the shopping bag." But even the first chaotic jottings stuffed into a bag as scraps "are the physical manifestation of the way my mind works, sparks flying off the wheel."

Carlson's rescued shopping bag is a perfect metaphor for all those bits we hide safely away till the right moment. The movie stubs or notations scribbled on an old concert program have all been saved to remind us of something in our lives. Often of others. It's the writing *about* others, though, that often keeps things hidden for years. Lifetimes. The shift from journals into creative work is more than moving writing from process to product. It's when we begin to move beyond the self to writing about the whole world. And writing one's own deeper stories inevitably involves writing directly about others.

The others in our lives. We're always fine until we get to *that* part of the memoir course. Suddenly, fifteen confident voices grind to a halt. While the character portrait is the last short narrative snapshot in my creative nonfiction courses, writing about others initially proves tricky for some. Doubt worms its way in; ambiguity breeds. The Censor is in heaven. After all, often it's others who've sent us scribbling in private diaries in the first place. Those maddening life companions — parents, spouses, children, lost loves, friends, relatives.

I stare at the class and tell them that one hard truth: to write about others is the first — not the final — step in beginning to see our own stories truly. It's the way to balance perspective. I remind them that they've been writing about others all along, just not consciously. Until the single incident snapshot showing a conflict, others have stayed as background. But even in journals, tone alone — longing, angry, hungry — is an important clue to locating where our stories and biases are about others. Tone is the temperature gauge showing us what we fear, what we desire. To write about another is always a double portrait: them and you. You by the very way you shape the story, settle on tone, decide what is or *isn't* told.

In writing about others, it's ourselves — not just them — who emerge in a newer, often truer, more complex light. Novelist and longtime journal keeper Mary Gordon discovered this in her memoir *The Shadow*

Man, about her intellectually ambitious father, who died when she was seven. At forty-four, while researching his life, she found that little of his story was true. His secrets forced her to reshape the narrative of her own life. Who was she? Still the adoring — and once adored — daughter whose confidence as a writer owed everything to the fictional success of her father's life? "What I had trusted as a text to live by," she writes, became "the shedding of illusion and the taking on of what may be another illusion, but one of my own."

The Other Faces in the Mirror

Two years ago a quiet older woman whose gray hair makes her eyes bluer joined my memoir class. Heidi White's decision to write about her father was easier than Gordon's. She greatly loved and admired his real accomplishments, and she had a dramatic story to tell: her father, a liberal Catholic journalist, had been part of a secret late attempt on Hitler's life. After the war, he survived to be elected to Germany's new government. By then, as he sketched his own memoir, Heidi had settled in New Haven with her American graduate student husband.

Forty years later, she decided to begin writing her version of her own childhood. (In her father's published memoir she was mentioned in only three paragraphs.) Writing a coming-of-age story set against a backdrop of pre- and postwar Germany, she wanted to capture a child's perspective of a heroic but absent father, a girl-hood spent grappling with his legacy. But how to fit her own story in while writing about others? Writing chronologically, she shifted from autobiography to memoir by capturing key turning points in her life in a series of snapshots: moving from city to city as her father lost his jobs for refusing to publish pro-Nazi articles; being hidden in a convent-run war hospital for a year, far away from her family; enduring the long trek alone back to Cologne after the war, living in a bombed-out apartment while losing a favorite brother to cancer.

Not just her father, but the war and the Nazi era itself also become characters in her book. All through the memoir's first draft, she reflected on how these his-toric events had shaped her as much as her family. To frame the memoir's opening, she went back to the object snapshot she'd done in her journal. It was a simple object — a pebble she'd picked up on a recent walk. It held the key to showing the arc of her life, well into her sixties: "When I close my fingers, its ragged edges dig into my skin. It's an ordinary gray stone with rusty red and black markings buried deep in its fissures.

When I hold this pebble I don't daydream as I do when touching the smooth piece of marble I found last year on the Greek island of Samos. Sometimes I hide the stone with the red blotches that look like dried blood under a pile of papers on my desk.

"I picked up the stone on a raw March day this year while strolling along the edge of Lake Wannsee in Berlin. As I bent down to pick up the pebble, I could see a group of houses on the opposite shore veiled in a gray mist. In one of them Hitler had signed the infamous Final Solution." She was in Berlin, nearly half a century later, as part of One-By-One, carrying on her father's social legacy by being part of a "dialogue between children of Holocaust survivors and descendants of the Third Reich." Framing the opening with her life's work allowed her to show how the war affected her long before she became a faculty wife in postwar America. In connecting the dots of her and others' stories, she made memory and meaning finally coalesce.

The Portrait Beneath the Portrait

Writing about others needs to be considered from two angles. The conflicts — fear of hurting others, the risk of exposing ourselves — are real. But so is the need to tell our own story — even if we never show it to anyone. That's much easier once we realize a subtle truth: *each* of us has created a personal version of the past. It may or may not correspond to how others experienced or remembered the same events. "The party was *not* for you, the spider was *not* a black widow," Joan Didion's family points out when comparing a shared memory. But it's our past, our version. As Patricia Hampl notes, "If we refuse to do the work of creating this personal version of the past, someone else will do it for us."

To begin to gain perspective on others, it's helpful to first do your *own* portrait. At midlife, Mary Gordon saw that it was herself, not her father, who needed to be seen anew. Anyone conflicted about portraying others should try this deceptively simple journal technique, which is best done by freewriting, often in a busy place so noise distracts you — and your Censor. Without pausing, quickly answer: How would your life — and you — have been different had you *not* known a particular person? (Often surprising is how adversity shapes character. At the very least, it provides endless material.) What is your single most important memory of them? How does that memory continue to influence your life? In what important ways are you different from the other? In what ways are you *like* them that you'd rather not acknowledge? What have you never told them? What would an outsider say of your relationship with the other?

That last question often evokes a response of either "loving" or "horrible." The truth is usually shaded somewhere in between. A solid portrait draws on several character angles. Memoir uses an important rule of fiction: always give even the worst character some redeemable trait or quality to make them believable. If a portrait is too angry or too falsely deferential, the *writer* as well as the story isn't credible.

There are several ways to get started when writing about others. Create a quick list of questions to spark specific details that are the core of character portraits. Others are first defined by what they desire, fear, and own. Here are a few examples: describe four things you'd find hidden in their medicine chest or bathroom drawer. Which food would they be most ashamed to be found eating? Describe a single outfit or article of clothing in their closet they've only worn once. Why? Describe a single object they'd never part with though it's long lost its meaning or value. Describe a single physical detail or gesture someone would notice if standing behind the person in a bank line. What is their most irritating gesture or mannerism? What nicknames trailed the person from childhood on?

If their voice (imagined or real) is silencing yours,

making it hard even to begin, write a scene involving you from *their* perspective. This is often a breakthrough technique. That was the case for someone whose older brother deliberately trashed her garden with his rusted cars. Telling it from his point of view, she had fresh insights: his shame at not being the success at work she was, his loneliness in not having a family. Her final portrait traced her lifelong guilt at not being able to help a gifted but lost brother, whose anger, she now realized, masked depression.

The greatest weapon in writing openly about others is also the one that heals: humor. (In two of my favorites memoirs, Tobias Wolff's *This Boy's Life* and Frank McCourt's *Angela's Ashes*, humor prevents self-pity but still catches the horrors of a rootless childhood.) A journal keeper conflicted over writing about her parents effortlessly wrote a character portrait of the family's one wildly humorous member: the trailer park grandmother. With the latest husband in tow, she cheats at Hearts or Monopoly, "drags out the first two letters of a word like 'blue' so that it sounds like *be-lue*," and ogles the groom at her granddaughter's wedding.

Culling journal details about the good-hearted schemer, the writer, Jayne Lacey, opened her portrait with an early memory: "On a sticky June day, a silver blue sedan with Florida license plates pulled into our cracked asphalt driveway. Stepping out of her dusty Ford onto a carpet of crabgrass, my grandmother ducked to avoid smashing her hairdo, stiff with Aqua-Net, which she wrapped each night in toilet paper. She was wearing a hot pink V-neck jersey and tight one-hundred-percent-elastic-waist-polyester pants. I imagined hearing my mother on the phone later complaining to her sister that 'Ma' should buy bigger-sized clothes, and while she was at it, a bra that fit."

Living to Tell the Tale

Crisis is often the catalyst for keeping a journal or beginning a memoir. Catherine Texier did both in a single year, the year in which more than her eighteen-year marriage fell apart. So did her work. Married to a fellow novelist, Texier also edited a literary journal with him from their New York home. "I couldn't control the circumstances of a man deciding if he was leaving me for someone else. But I could control words." The diary, "like a documentary," gave her distance on an ever-shifting marriage. Late at night she typed journal entries into her computer. She watched the journal's focus slowly shift away from wanting to hang on to the marriage or salvage the literary partnership. The deeper story that emerged was of how she tried to make life normal for their two daughters while reinventing herself at midlife.

Often with him in another room, she'd write in the diary what she couldn't show out of fear of losing him: confusion, neediness, fear. "From the start, I wrote it to him. But about a month in, the *you* switched to *he*. I knew a narrative was emerging." The journal was her lifeline. A published novelist, Texier instinctively knew how to shape and cut scenes emerging in journal entries. She let details show the contradictory impulses of a separating couple: waiting all night for him to return, making love but feeling only the heat of sexual loss.

Texier's *Breakup*, a memoir as diary, chronicles the slow stages of a family caught in slow-motion crossfire. Initially, anger gave her license to think of publishing. But deciding to turn diary into memoir forced Texier to tap "a more universal story than being a cast-off wife. Self-portrait as victim only obscures the real story. It's less a portrait of him or even myself than of anyone at a certain stage of life who redefines control. Control, in my case, meant sitting until I knew it was the right moment to let go." That, as Texier told me on a New York street corner recently, was what allowed her to accept the end of the marriage. Now, as the two improvise a healthy parenting partnership, she is glad she left a trace of how that became possible.

Mimicking Memory Itself

Memoirs, like journals, often mimic the way memory works: shifting back and forth between past and present, trying to link event and meaning. In her celebrated memoir, *Girl, Interrupted*, about two years in a mental ward for teenage girls, Susanna Kaysen deliberately fractured the story's time line to mirror memory itself. Writing twenty years later, she began by sketching a series of two-to-four-page narrative snapshots, in lieu of the diary she wasn't able to keep at the time. (Kaysen, as anyone who knows her well can tell you, has a photographic memory; she's able to invoke scenes whole, improvising only dialogue.)

Kaysen fit the scenes onto notecards. When finally ready to structure the memoir, she placed the cards on the floor, intentionally scrambling scenes. Subtly ordered, the memoir lets readers experience the chaotic humor and horror of institutional life. The real trick, though, was writing with sharp-eyed compassion for her wardmates while neatly omitting details about her own family. To discover clues to her childhood, Kaysen forces readers to do detective work, studying details hidden in her official case file, which is threaded throughout the memoir. "People ask, How did you get in there? What they really want to know is if they are likely to end up in there as well," she writes. "All I can tell them is, It's easy."

The shifting shadow play of memory wasn't just a way for Helen Fremont to structure her eloquently moving memoir, *After Long Silence.* Memory itself was at the core of her family's story. Her parents' willful silence about their background puzzled Fremont growing up. To solve the mystery behind this silence was somehow to solve her family's — and her own — identity. As a child, Fremont was taught to make the sign of the cross. Her European war refugee parents raised her Catholic. Only in time did she discover from others that they were in fact Holocaust survivors.

Fremont directly took on the challenge of writing about herself, her parents, her aunt. It wasn't easy. As she traveled and interviewed family about her mother and aunt's Eastern European childhood, she soon became immersed in the interplay of memory and shifting story perspectives. "Secrecy and denial were essential components of my family, and by the time I was finally able to piece together my own history, my need to speak the truth was enormous. I didn't want to violate my family's privacy, nor to exploit their stories for my own use, but I needed, at last, to be able to speak."

Scenes first sketched in notebooks slowly grew into a memoir. Fremont says, "It took me over six years to write my memoir, and most of that time I spent agonizing over whether I had the right to write the book. I questioned my motives daily. I judged myself harshly. For months at a time, I quit writing altogether, terrified of my family's anticipated reaction. And yet, I knew that if I didn't write this book, what I would lose, I think, would be myself. I needed to set down my understanding of my own world on the page in order that I not be erased from it."

Secrecy's legacy is explored in a crucial area of her own life, not just her family's. In the memoir's twin narrative, Fremont traces moving from childhood silence to adult voice, claiming her own sexual identity. "At the heart of writing," she says, "vital to our sense of connection, is the desire to let our thoughts emerge and live in the world." If writing the memoir achieved that for her, so did it too for countless readers who experienced shocks of recognition in her stories. Truths deeper than her own family's history surfaced. The human need to fill in omissions, to bridge worlds hidden in the cramped spaces of invented narratives, is the greater story.

Writing about others was the only vehicle for Fremont. "I tried to record what I knew, and then questioned how I knew those things. The same story can be told a thousand ways, and the choices we make about how we tell ourselves stories — and how we tell our story — say so much about how our imagination and memory contribute, ultimately, to our identity." The greatest reward, she told me, "is my recent discovery of an extended family that I never knew existed. My book has brought us together after fifty years of silence."

Stepping Back from the Story

Like the two seemingly identical drawings I'd study as a child, what's missing in a story is often as interesting as what's left in, especially when writing about others. Memoirs consciously do what diaries do unconsciously: omit things. A journal, unintentionally, lies by omission. Diarists simply can't hold the whole truth of a day. That fuller truth is only seen in retrospect, often years later. Memoir is the deliberate shaping of that final truth. Is every single detail in most memoirs true? I doubt it. Time is compressed, scenes are shaped into narrative, characters are given details culled from years of memory. "The crucial distinction for me is not the difference between fact and fiction," says Toni Morrison, "but the distinction between fact and truth."

Ironically, the inability to keep a diary honestly works to a creative writer's advantage. Reshaping material satisfies the itch to blur lines, contour a story and find the larger emotional truth at its center. Memoir doesn't reconstruct the world but interprets it; the known becomes transformed. Both journals and memoirs inevitably set out to solve a question about identity — one's own and others' — revealing the obstacles along the way. Crafting narrative snapshots into memoir, a journal keeper takes a lesson from what every fiction writer knows firsthand: the story is often told backward. Or at least by opening with a dramatic incident, as Heidi White did with herself in her sixties, eyeing Hitler's Berlin headquarters, picking up a pebble to remind herself of a lost childhood.

To step back and see material clearly, though, means being ruthless in knowing the clichés of your subject. Susanna Kaysen subverts our expectations about a mental ward, for example, by writing with fierce clarity — and humor. Writing about his con-man father — who kept cars taken out for test drives and had the tooth fairy leave I.O.U. notes — Geoffrey Wolff (Tobias's brother) crafts a black valentine of a memoir, *The Duke of Deception*. "One day, writing about my father with no want of astonishment and love, it came to me that I am his creature as well as his get. I cannot now shake this conviction, that I was trained as his instrument of perpetuation, put here to put him into the record."

"Hell, get it off your chest," Mary Karr's mother told her, knowing she was writing about her spiritedly dysfunctional childhood in her memoir, *The Liars' Club*. "She accepted my child's-eye view of history as inherently valid, perhaps because, as a young art student in New York, she'd studied perspective, how appearances shift depending on where the artist stands."

After the success of *The Liars' Club*, Karr contacted fellow memoirists who'd hazarded into writing publicly about others. Had everyone survived? In his copy of *The Woman Warrior*, Maxine Hong Kingston's father wrote elaborate commentary on her memories of family life. He wrote it as poetry, an art he'd abandoned on leaving China three decades earlier. Years later, seeing his annotated copy displayed in a glass case at a literary reception, "he said loudly in English, so that other onlookers could hear, 'My writing!'"

EXERCISES AND JOURNAL PROMPTS

⌒ Divide a page top to bottom. Do a thumbnail sketch of yourself at ten-year intervals on the left-hand side. Do the same sketch process of someone else, placing those paragraphs on the right. Underline overlapping key life moments. What were each person's responses to those moments? How have they continued to define the relationship between you and another?

- Ask three people who have known you for a long period to write you a one-page letter describing what you were like at certain stages in your life. It provides instant perspective.

- Poet Maria Kraus often writes letters in journals to others no longer in her life. Some have died; others have simply moved away. To continue a dialogue deepens our understanding of others and their role in our lives. Write to the mother who died, now that you're a parent. Or to the teacher whose name you forget but who first started you on your career.

- Make a list of all the clichés associated with the subject you've written about. Go back through a draft and see how it avoided or fell into clichés, especially the trap of sentimentality. Begin then to look for a central thematic pattern, or motif, that links the stories.

CHAPTER XI

Leaving a Trace: A Past Regained, a Future Imagined

❧

I have found so many sides of myself in the diaries of others. I would like it if I someday reflect future readers to themselves, provide them with examples, warnings, courage, and amusement. In these unedited glimpses of the self in others, of others in the self, is another of the covenants posterity makes with the day-to-day.

—Gail Godwin

"As a young college innocent I used to hand current journals over to new beaux so they could 'understand' me. *Poor* guys." As she tells this, her face full of mock horror, Marcia Deihl throws her hands wide in the air, as if warding off the folly. It's an unwritten code: to announce that you keep a journal is like announcing a vice; neither are meant to be public. "I now may choose to show a close friend a section of a past journal, but the current one is surrounded by a force field of protection."

Marcia, who works in one of Harvard's libraries, is telling stories about moving from private journals to published work one sultry late-summer afternoon in the home of Hope Hale Davis. Hope is ninety-six. She looks a decade younger than eighty-two, the age she began teaching journal and writing classes in Cambridge, Massachusetts, guiding generations of writers. Her creative energy is closer to thirty-two, her age when her first stories were published in *The New Yorker*.

We are seated at her oval walnut dining room table, which is laden with Hope's journals, their margins a bright zigzag of Post-its. Though Hope has carefully selected them, it feels like a kind of high-stakes chess game. In a way it is. Hope is sharing sections from years of journals. As she opens the first, she trains her bemused but fiercely astute intelligence on me. She seems to look straight through me; it's as if, by telepathy, she's already read the diary entry I'll write about her the next morning.

She begins, each Post-it like the flap of an advent calendar, opening a new window on her life: her early writing career; years of political commitment; literary life with her professor husband, who taught Norman Mailer at Harvard and Sylvia Plath at Smith College. The pages are beautifully written, full of what she tells journal classes to do — pack in closely observed details. As she reads, whole worlds emerge: lunch with Hemingway's wife; winter-afternoon games with her children; stories from her own memoir, *Great Day Coming*, published when she was ninety-one.

All afternoon the real subject is the writing life. For the three of us seated at the table, publication has happened at different stages. But this we share in common: in moving from journals to published work, the catalyst is often a group of readers helping along the way. Both Hope and I had Marcia in courses. "From the start," Marcia says, "Hope's name was a kind of omen. I entered with twenty-six years of journals. Over time, she led me to see how to draft my version of my life, not that of my parents, lovers, or friends. I learned to use my diaries to name myself, to discover the writing craft, which, I learned from her own life, often improves with age."

Still writing each morning just before work, Marcia refers to journals at night "when I want to check my real life, not my imagined life." It's always been the case. "My first journal was an insurance company calendar my dad gave me. I started on January 1, a third of a page a day. For years, I used the same calendar. At the bottom, it had weights and measures, height and weight charts." They were private emblems in a private diary. If Marcia hadn't been in a memoir class of mine, I'd never have guessed weight was an issue that had plagued her. Like a diary, she has a sleek exterior. But when she was growing up, life was more like being inside a private journal, where she wrote "the uncensored (if coded) truth" about the misery of a world that often defines identity solely by body image. "I started keeping a diary at thirteen, when I weighed one-eighty, as recorded by the school nurse (out loud, as I remember)."

Success at school didn't change that inner image. "Having always felt myself a misfit confused by peer pressure, I was a non-cheerleader type in a small town." A year after college, Marcia's favorite cousin, Suzanne, came to stay for six months. On a whim, they decided to share portions of old journals. At first they picked the same days in their journals to compare how each had experienced the world. Marcia found an early entry. December 1965: "Teenagers are supposed to love parties and social life, but I HATE IT. It's mostly that I don't have any close friends. I'm down to 163."

As her cousin listened to excerpts, Marcia's perspective sharpened. A story unfolded about how overweight kids "live in a world of exile," hearing "the sad sigh of a beautiful mother who, once again, pins up her daughter's size-eighteen hem." Kids who "feel the raw burns on the hands after other kids shinny up the rope in gym class, you still hanging there, a teacher taking pity, giving a C for effort" and who "remember the look of disgust in their sixth-grade dance partner."

The diary itself, but also the sharing of its stories, gave her distance, reshaping her self-image. Literally. After sharing the stories with a trusted listener, Marcia began writing seriously and shed fifty pounds. Since then she's kept a series of single-focus diaries ("currently in pretty awful, carpal-tunnel longhand"). "As a diarist who's written a page a day since January 1, 1963, I can only say it feels more like a compulsion than a discipline." The discipline of writing, though, transformed her. On a recent visit home, she went back sleek, confident, published. "At my high school's twenty-fifth reunion, I read *highly* censored parts of my high school journal and had people rolling on the floor. This time, it wasn't just me who got insights into how once-fat girls behave."

One for All

Joyce Carol Oates thinks of her journal as a tree the earth divides into two galaxies: the trunk, "a visible but seemingly infinite little galaxy of limbs," matched by "its root system: an invisible twin galaxy of branches hidden in the earth." In short, the conscious and unconscious parts of oneself. The same two worlds apply to writers, "with what is called the 'social self' and the 'private self.' The self 'out there' (seen and known by others) and the self 'in here' (never seen and never known — at least by others)."

Those two galaxies merge when moving from a journal into creative work. Often a group gives a writer permission the individual has long denied himself. Strangely, the final stage of journal keeping for many is moving their stories into a world of sympathetic but sharp-eyed readers. To be part of a writing group, says Hope Hale Davis, "is to take responsibility for others. It means playing detective to work other than your own." No matter how tiny, such groups are about problem solving. To find an honest but trusted core of readers is to enter into a contract with a writer, listening, finding what's already working in early stages of drafts, showing where the subconscious has left invaluable clues. "In a good working group," says Hope, "confidence and voice emerge, not just dozens of drafts."

While most keep diaries to silence their Censor, ironically, it's a group that can free the writer of the Censor altogether. How? "No matter how much others nitpick," says Hope, "you quickly see that you're hardest on your own work. *I* still am. At ninety-six, you'd think you'd be over it, but a good writer always has more doubts than confidence." Katya Taylor runs small writing groups, but to spark her own work, she turns to her friend Sara, whom she met at a book discussion group in 1996. Since then, they often write together for an hour, using "seed phrases to kick-start our creativity."

Solitude, a journal writer's necessity, can also isolate a writer. A group not only shatters that isolation, it provides the confidence to *return* to solitude. "It's a writing, not a talking, group," says Katya Taylor of her own. "Listening is witnessing — you are there to honor the process, not to compare it with your own." To get started in larger groups, she picks "a single word or seed phrase as a springboard into longer work. As someone chooses to read, others just listen. Witnessing." Why do it? "There are no distractions, there's a timed period, say a half hour, in which creativity can surface." That's exactly what happened for three journal keepers in Carmel, California. Julie Houy, Joan Miller, and Carolyn Livingston met in a writing class for senior citizens. Soon they formed their own group. Their first mystery, *Beyond Bingo,* written collectively, was just published.

Just as Anne Frank imagined an ideal reader for her diary, sharing writing with others helps us imagine an audience beyond ourselves. A group automatically reframes a journal's stories, helping the writer to see both the writing and the material differently. "The very stories I was terrified to tell," says Marcia Deihl, "were the ones people liked best. Setting context forced me to see stories through others' eyes. With each draft, others helped me to that final clarity." Deborah Weisgall takes it a step further. While writing her recent memoir, *A Joyful Noise,* about her composer father, she printed drafts "in a hideous font so you can't be seduced by the familiar look of a published page. A strange font really makes you resee." Similarly, essayist Sven Birkerts makes bad, grainy photocopies of his work to defamiliarize the writing for final drafts.

"No marks on paper," says novelist Mary Gordon, "can ever measure up to the music in the mind, to the purity of language before its ambush by language." *Giving* the Censor work is a journal's final transformation. While waiting for meaning to surface in memoir, tackle the writing. If you can't revise a knotty psychological issue, revise sentences instead. "Use more red!" Hope Hale Davis admonishes. As a group zeroes in on language, cutting and shaping prose, the Censor at last becomes an ally. "I want the truth of the stories, not the false cover of obscuring language," says Marcia Deihl.

Redrafting the Self

Journal writing has always been a form of witnessing for award-winning concert pianist Linda Cutting. When she was at a Colorado girls' camp at twelve, she relates, "our counselor sent us off with Bible, notebooks, and pencil to hunt for a private place to commune with God." On a European college tour, she "wrote in an old church graveyard while leaning against a tombstone identified by a framed black-and-white photograph of a young dark-haired girl nailed into the stone like a warning." While she stayed at a convent where nuns asked visitors to draw a sin from a basket, "The sin I drew was pride, but my real sin was hiding from the group to write in secret. I confessed both sins in my journal, and kept writing."

In graduate school, "I spent hours practicing the piano, preparing for concerts and competitions, but always with a journal beside me." Then the journals' focus shifted. "I began writing daily, almost desperately, after my oldest brother killed himself. I kept a one-sided correspondence to keep him alive." When she was twenty-eight, her remaining brother committed suicide. "My parents asked me to lie about his death, to say it had been an accident." Cutting soon began having memory slips during concerts, missing musical passages. The slips were linked to childhood silences she began probing, finally remembering deeper family secrets.

"I needed the support of friends who knew the shattering truth, but I also desperately needed to tell that truth." I met her at that point when we were in the same writing group. While her journals had become "a record of memories threatened with extinction," she told us of "the growing family pressure to annihilate the real stories." Over two years, as she turned a shelf of journals into her poignantly redemptive memoir, *Memory Slips,* the group offered a kind of sanctuary.

Relying on the journals, Cutting first wrote under the protective cover of fiction. The story, she realized, needed to be told directly, as nonfiction memoir. Claiming the inherent power of her real life story allowed her to tap its more universal message: the need and freedom to tell the truth, even if it means standing up to family. Cutting's decision was a crucial transformation in a writing life. "With a pen to mark the shape of memories," writing became a spiritual claim, she observed. Her first step was an autobiographical essay, which the *New York Times* published to wide acclaim.

The first-person account of family silence around physical and sexual abuse hit a deep public chord. As she turned the piece into a full-length memoir, she gained support from the group, which helped Cutting sustain the courage to tell the deeper truths: "What was once protected inside journals, locked in basement filing cabinets, later stored on open shelves in my study, was eventually sifted and sorted and opened for public viewing as a book."

Lovers and Other Strangers

In her novel *The Golden Notebook*, Doris Lessing writes about lovers who keep two diaries: one the other can read; the second, a secret one. One lover can't resist reading the other's secret diary, dooming the relationship. While with suicidal intimacy Tolstoy and his wife read their diaries for forty-one years, many first turn to family before finding outside readers. Where's the balance between privacy and sharing work emerging from journals?

First showing work is a very delicate balancing act. "I can't fire my Censor," a retired judge once told me. "I'm *married* to him." Yet Donna Stein says of her dream and creative notebooks, "When I first met my husband, he read some of them. 'This is the real you,' he said. 'This is what you should write like,' when I told him I wanted to be a writer. He still says they're among the best things I've ever written." It gave her the confidence to find a serious writing group.

New York literary agent Betsy Lerner and her husband have kept journals since childhood. They met in college at a writers' salon held by "a self-styled Gertrude Stein with a bowl haircut and a pink refrigerator." When they married, Betsy was terrified she'd read *his* journals. And not for the poetry each wrote. "I'd already made one such foray before we lived together and I feared I might strike again." They bought a locked filing cabinet with separate drawers. "Once we got it home, my husband pulled a move that changed the nature of our marriage. He dropped the keys in his desk and said he wasn't going to use the cabinet. He said he wanted to trust me." While they share creative and business work, the journals remain private on open shelves.

Some of the best readers of emerging journal stories are newly reconstituted family, groups that have come together in retirement or nursing homes. "At this point," says a retired Florida writer, "you've learned to be direct, to know what counts in life, which is honesty and generosity, helping someone see life's stories clearly. Tell the tale." Freed of the fear of hurting immediate family, it's often easier to share stories openly. While many now regret burning diaries after marriage or before going into a home, new journals trigger stories never told in the originals. The group is collective memory. "The journals," as one woman told me, "hold the stories of those who've been here, remembered long after us."

Lost Diaries, Preserved Memories

In the summer between Samantha Harvey's junior and senior years at Harvard, the storage bin in her dorm was broken into. Nearly twenty volumes of diaries were lost. She posted a reward, no questions asked. Seven months later, she imagined the diaries in a Dumpster somewhere. "I could almost see them buried in a heap, the ink running down the pages. Yet I felt strangely calm." The next day the dorm superintendent called; someone had left them outside his office. "I spent the rest of the afternoon just touching them. I opened one page that described a visit to a villa in Umbria, spending a warm summer evening on a veranda, peeling slices of nectarine and soaking them in my wineglass. This small moment, lost otherwise to memory, was preserved on one page in the diary. I felt like an amnesiac whose memory was restored."

Walking down Boston's Marlborough Street one night last summer, Pamela Painter told me her idea: a security warehouse where, for a small fee, you could safely send your journals. We'd been talking about her published short story "Historical Necessity," inspired after a friend's car had been broken into, her diary stolen. Painter sympathized with the loss. Years ago, as her own marriage unraveled, she was afraid to have her journals in the house. Only she knew which pages were drafts of stories, which were real-life ones for no one's eyes. She gave the journals to a close friend for safe-keeping. While the friend was moving, the diaries got lost.

The short story, based on a friend's recent journal loss, creatively transformed her own. In it, Painter imagined the journal's new group of readers — not the boys who'd stolen the car, but the girlfriend of one of them, who'd taken it to her trailer park home.

The girl would be annoyed by the sloppy handwrit-ing and periodically get up to try a new eyeshadow. Perhaps Ceily's highschool picture that she used as a placemark would fall out and there'd she be — large brown eyes, round face and long straight hair, little changed — on the dusty trailer floor. The next night there would be an improvisational reading at the All-

Night Diner while her friends sat around listening. The girl would express amazement at how she disliked the exact same things about her own mother. Ceily pictured them whispering together, leaning toward each other over thin hamburgers and shiny french fries as if close to the punch line of a dirty joke. She pictured them reading her analysis of how Harry's love-making changed, of how his big hands and feet, which were at first terribly erotic to her, now seemed the appendages of some strange heavy animal. Once as he slept and before she left for the theater, she stood and looked down at them hanging over the edge of her flowered sheets. It was a little thing to notice. But wasn't that what journals were for?

The journal finally ends up in a man's hands, but before then the girls "would read certain passages aloud in turn. Certain ones they read alone, passing the journal around — finally beginning to suspect that sex was supposed to feel good, to last longer than two minutes and needn't take place in stolen cars. Ceily imagined one of the girls secretly buying a green stenographer's pad and starting a journal of her own."

Unlike in Pam Painter's short story, a friend returned Michelle Cheuk's journals. A cardboard box with a dozen spiral notebooks arrived shortly before she headed east for college. In the box were dozens of her old journals. First begun as letters, the journals were written for a single reader: Michelle's closest school girlfriend. Her friend loved reading another's journals. A perfectionist, though, she refused to share her own. (She'd used scissors on her earliest secret journals.) As Michelle gained "fluency, confidence and voice," her friend retreated to silence, finally cutting off the friendship, too. When she did, she returned Michelle's journals, carefully placing a single rose on the thousands of words that had come into the world.

The Final Fate of One's Journals

"And thus ends all that I doubt I shall ever be able to do with my own eyes in the keeping of my journall," Samuel Pepys ended his famous diary as he went blind. His diaries, preserved for posterity, have never been out of print. What life, if any, will one's own journals have? Worried about leaving writing that may hurt others or leave a false impression, some consider burning a lifetime of journals. Those who have all tell me it's one of the greatest regrets of their lives.

Here at the turn of the new millennium, there are no such inhibitions for thousands who post diary entries daily on the Internet, on sites like Open Pages or Metajournals. An exhibitionist's or voyeur's paradise, public airwaves now buzz with private thoughts. But as an entry can be erased in an icy electronic blip, for many the need is simply to connect, find an audience for writing, shatter isolation. In the end, it's not privacy or secrecy that most people say haunts them when they think of journals. It's not leaving a trace. Permanence, not secrecy, guides them.

Journals, though, often have a fickle fate. A caller to "The Connection," a radio program in Boston, told me of finding a journal left in the apartment she'd rented. A two-year record of a young man's experience in the Peace Corps, the journal so intrigued and moved her she couldn't let it sit in a drawer. With detective work from clues in the diary, she tracked down the writer, who was living in South America. The two now have a long, unbroken correspondence.

After his father's death, Marcus Rosenbaum, a senior producer for National Public Radio, traveled to Florida, "with the bittersweet task of cleaning out the family home." His niece, rummaging in a front bed-room closet, retrieved a journal. "The leather was cracking. And although the stitching in the binding was coming undone, the pages had scarcely yellowed." It was a 1910 daybook his grandmother, Helen Jacobus Apte, had begun upon her marriage. The journal, like a companion, guided him through the twentieth century. He saw both World Wars, the Depression, the return of Halley's Comet through her sharp eyes. But "like the heroine of a Victorian novel, she chose duty over desire." The diary was also an internal compass, pointing to struggles in love, showing there are no ordinary days, no ordinary lives. Rosenbaum edited the diary, published as *Heart of a Wife*, of the southern grandmother he'd only met once.

What is a journal's final fate? To whom are we to leave them? A journal, begun alone, is often destined to end up with others: family, friends, landlord. Like Pepys, who donated his journals to his college at Cambridge, many journal writers seek permanence in library or archive collections. As journals are often the first step in documenting a creative life, many writers consider leaving them to special collections. Others include clauses in wills, dictating who can or can't read the journals. It's a Solomon-like decision process. A woman announced she was leaving her extensive journal collection to a specific granddaughter. Why, her daughters wondered, not to each of them? Why not copies to the whole family? Why exclude the male grandchildren?

Ask others who they wish had kept a diary and the answer is always one's immediate family. Some are lucky to have even a single journal. "My sister kept a journal off and on until her death in a small plane crash in 1981," says Lisa Colt. "I treasure the one volume that survives. It covers a year near the end of her life. Escaping the aftermath of a painful divorce, she was living and working in Teheran during the last days of the Shah. Graceful line drawings of a neighbor's cat are interwoven with her passionate longings for home and children. Details of angry Iranian student demonstrations are interspersed with notes on the books she is reading. When I open my sister's journal, it's as if I'd invited her into the room with me."

Throughout her childhood, Terri Evans recalls how her father retreated to his den, "shedding his daytime skin as a defense analyst." There he read and wrote for pleasure, not publication. "Of his journals my sister and I knew little other than that they were his evening's chosen companion." A few days after her father died, she sat and read his journals. "I was stunned by what I read. There, neatly chronicled in three-ring binders, was my father's life, from college and the Second World War, through his marriage and my mother's death." But, she realized, "the man who was my father revealed a more complex portrait of a man in the context of his time." In its pages he had interwoven his personal reflections and observations of the larger world. "An entry about my first-grade Thanksgiving play, followed by the news of President Kennedy's assassination; the science fair and Resurrection City; the senior prom and Saigon falling. The look of Washington after the 1968 riots. In his journals he had set our lives against the backdrop of the world." Among the journals was a passage from a letter he'd written her in college. She found it again decades later. On sustaining inspiration, he wrote, "Guard it well; respect it. And if you lose it for an hour, or a day, never forget that it is merely waiting to be rediscovered." Having his journals allowed her to heed his words now in a more meaningful way.

A New England minister once confessed he'd lost his journal in a subtler way: by never writing his past down in a journal. In midlife, he wanted a record for himself as much as for his family. Someone else told me of the few photographs she has of her father. She searches for him in the small traces he left: familiar handwriting on the back of faded photos. "I study the handwriting over and over, as if hieroglyphics." These are lives stolen by silence. A woman who called in to a Washington, D.C., radio show told me a story that haunts me. Until her mother's death, she never knew that her mother had kept a journal. The daughter discovered it hidden in old insurance files. A day after the funeral, she read the journal in a single sitting. Instead of the cold, bitter mother she'd known, another self presented her case to posterity: she wrote about the love she couldn't express in life, exploring why, airing her frustration at a thwarted creative career.

That day the daughter both lost and regained her mother. "If I had known what I learned from her journal, saw the world through her eyes, it would have changed our entire relationship. It came too late for us in life, but I'm strangely grateful, as it's gotten me to keep some record for my own children. Sitting in that attic, I learned that there are always many, not just two sides, of the same story."

Transforming the Legacy

As I glance now at my shelves of journals, I'm struck by all the still-untold stories — notes, fragments, details — waiting to coalesce into stories. On the far right-hand shelf, next to my first half-filled childhood diaries, sits my grandmother's Red Cross album journal. I smile at the irony: of all the many journals in my family, it's my grandmother's alone that sits prominently on the shelf. In a fit of cleaning in between moves, my mother tossed out her weepy early marriage journals. My aunt's decades of journals are with her. Struggling with Parkinson's disease, she pecks patiently at a special keyboard her computer-whiz son invented for her, while her daughter edits the two novels that sprang from five decades of journals.

When I look at that Red Cross photo album journal, I see far more than its faded blue cloth cover tattered at the edges. I see it as my passport to becoming a writer. My grandmother, the only family member careful not to leave a trace in writing, spurred me to do just that. By giving me her journal in my twenties, she tacitly gave me permission to solve its omissions. From childhood on, I'd memorized each photo, connecting it to the larger story of my grandmother's life: meeting my grandfather on the ship to Japan and Russia (but late in the voyage, as she was often seasick, surfacing only the final week); riding in vans over frozen Siberian waters to remote medical outposts; caring for half-starved war prisoners for a year; receiving the telegram in which my grandfather proposed; arriving six months later in San Francisco, the quay dotted with the tiny figures of her future sisters-in-law, those terrifying women — principals with schools named after them, legal activists who championed immigrant naturalization rights.

There is no photo in the album of her first staring down at those stylishly hatted women. No photo of her expression as she reflected on marrying into that tight-knit, literate, Irish-American family, its members sharp-eyed, opinionated, competitive. And despite later photos showing her doing prenatal medicine in New York before she had her own children, there are none that capture the look I often saw when someone cross-examined her about her childhood. The eyes tightened. No amount of competence could undo the fact that, from earliest memory, she felt herself an outsider.

After walking down that ship's gangplank, my grandmother never again kept a journal. But I did.

Skipping a generation, my journal filled in what hers never recorded: that she'd spent seventeen years, not six, as she claimed, in an orphanage rife with humiliations; that her "loving aunts" were merely a series of foster families who shuttled her back at whim; that, at nineteen, she lied about her age to be admitted to medical training; that, after marriage, with her penchant bordering on arson for lighting candles at Mass, she blended in as a Catholic, but wasn't born one; that, dying, months after turning ninety-four, her final words called out for her own lost mother, Emma Zelman.

Omissions. Lies. Stories. Truth. While these were what she looked for in obituaries, they were what I listened for in her, just as I studied those two seemingly identical drawings in the children's section of the newspaper. As my eye scanned the drawings, trying to find the items omitted in one, I realized my grandmother was teaching me how to make connections. How to listen. How to observe the world. The real gift she was giving me, though, was the legacy of imagination, of knowing how to transform stubborn facts into stories, how to recognize that the story not told is often the most interesting one. How every story — and life — is of value.

She may not have left written journals, but she produced three generations after her who would. As my mother starts a journal again in her early seventies, my aunt continues hers begun in her twenties; my cousin, the zoologist, guides her own two children, helping them keep nature journals.

As I write this, the study floor is piled with stacks of journals others have lent me. Nearby is Lisa Colt's tiny watercolor self-portraits with pen-and-ink side commentaries; under it, her ship captain grandfather's "tiny cardboard log, illustrated with wobbly pencil sketches"; his wife's daybook tersely announces Lisa's father's birth. In another stack is a June 21, 1971, entry from Jim Cummings's forty-eight years of journals. Next to ten photocopied pages from Ray Zager's decades of indexed journals is M. Elaine Mar's reflections on the calligraphy journals in which she recorded ancestors' names as a child. In her own first private journal, "I didn't want the pages to curl from the heat of my palms, didn't want the spine to crack in places where I'd opened it, didn't want my handwriting to clutter its pages." Years later, though, pages in college journals stretched into a published memoir on those ancestors. Samantha Harvey, taking time off from Cambridge to train for the Olympics, just recently sent me the only thing she had time to record yesterday in her journal. "The feel of my blue Waterman fountain pen, which has traveled all around the world with me, the physicality of the journals themselves, of all different sizes and shapes, represents the real texture of everyday life."

I glance at the floor piled high with stacks of these and other journals and think of all the stories that over time will come into being: millions of words, invisible galaxies within each.

Acknowledgments

Virginia Woolf once observed that a book never comes into the world completely by itself. I want to thank, first and foremost, all those who shared journals and their stories with me over the years. *Leaving a Trace* owes much to the generosity of individuals, who range from close friends to callers to National Public Radio, to former students and fellow journal keepers. I am particularly grateful to those who interrupted not only busy lives, but ones often in adversity: Nancy Kline, for example, caring for an ailing mother, who took time to share how discovering her mother's journal affected writing her own novel; Audrey Lee calmly corresponding about homelessness; Suzanne Weeks reflecting on journals in between cancer treatments.

All these stories owe their permanence to two wonderful people: my agent, Elaine Markson; and above all, my editor, Sarah Burnes, an inspiring editor, truly a privilege to work with.

And ongoing thanks to my Tuesday night writer's group, to my husband, Askold, and to my family.